Profits from Dream Pillows

Jim Long

Edited by Joshua Young

Copyright© 1997

Jim Long

All rights reserved. The contents of this book may not be reproduced in any manner, by print or electronically, without specific written permission from the author.

Exceptions: Pages noted as patterns, or with information for copying (header tag, package insert, pattern), are meant to be photocopied for the use of the purchaser of this book and permission is given to photocopy, scan or photograph those pages only for the specific purpose of using them as original artwork for header tag labels and inserts.

Long Creek Herbs
P.O. Box 127
Blue Eye, Missouri 65611

ISBN 1-889791-12-1

Contents

Introduction
Discovering Dream Pillows
Page 3

Chapter 1
Why Dream Pillows Work
Page 7

Chapter 2
Herbs for Dream Pillows
Page 10

Chapter 3
Things to Consider, Making the Pillow & Sources
Page 26

Chapter 4
Jim's Secret Formulas
Page 31

Chapter 5
Packaging, Sources & Originals
Page 41

Chapter 6
Marketing Your Pillows & More Resources
Page 51

Introduction
Discovering Dream Pillows

When customers, both retail and wholesale, see what a substantial percentage of my business is devoted to dream pillows they occasionally seem surprised. "Do you really sell all of these?" they will ask.

Not only do I sell "all of these," but I've succeeded with dream pillows, in part because for me, they have worked.

I was first introduced to dream pillows by Jerry Stamps, a pharmacist friend of mine, in 1980. I was struggling with depression that was the result of a divorce and separation from my children.

I was unable to sleep, and when sleep did come, there were nightmares. I sought help, first from a doctor, who gave me a prescription for an anti-depressant, then from my pharmacist friend. He looked at my prescription and said, "This is going to make you groggy and diminish your ability to work for a few days. Would you like an alternative?" He suggested, "You need a dream pillow and some valerian capsules."

He explained valerian is an herb that relaxes muscles and that dream pillows are a very old craft based upon how fragrance effects memory.

He made a little cloth pillow, about 2 inches across and 4 inches long and filled it with mugwort and lavender. When he handed it to me he said, "Put this in your pillowcase where you will inhale the very subtle fragrances as you sleep. People have been using this mixture for centuries and it may possibly help you."

He further told me to take a couple of valerian capsules about 30 minutes before bedtime, saying the valerian would relax me and the pillow should keep the nightmares away. Over several nights I began to see improvement and told him my results.

"I'm not surprised," he said. "It's pretty amazing how fragrances, even very subtle ones, can effect our mind and dreaming."

My next introduction to dream pillows came about 4 years

later when I was staying in the Ozarks mountain home of writer and plant authority, Billy Joe Tatum. In her home during an extended visit while I was working on the Heritage Herb Garden at the Ozarks Folk Center, I had been waking each morning with the memory of another horrendous nightmare from the previous night. I began telling my host at breakfast about the previous night's frightening dream.

Finally one morning she said, "I'll bet there's a bad dream pillow up there in your sleeping space. After breakfast we'll check to see."

When the dishes were washed and put away she and I went upstairs and began looking through the numerous throw pillows around the bed where I slept. Sure enough we found a little bag, about 3 inches by 4 inches, filled with herbs. My host carried it downstairs and emptied out the contents onto a newspaper on the table.

"I can easily see why you were having nightmares," Billy Joe said. "This isn't a dream pillow blend. Someone has mistakenly filled the bag with potpourri. Potpourri should never be used in a dream pillow."

She pointed out several plants that she said should not be used in a dream blend. There were French marigold blossoms, bay leaves, Russian false tarragon, sage and tansy leaves and several more herbs.

"Unless you are making a mixture specifically for nightmares and to cause headaches, these herbs should not ever be used this way," she concluded, making the point again.

I was impressed. With the dream pillow that my pharmacist friend Jerry had made, I had discounted its usefulness as simply the power of suggestion. He said it would work and I wanted to believe it; therefore, it worked.

But this was different. I hadn't known the mis-mixed dream pillow was even in my sleeping quarters. But I definitely had been having very colorful, very disturbing dreams. (And other guests who had slept in that space also later reported unusually disturbing dreams when they had stayed there).

I began to research dream pillows and found that they had been called "comfort pillows" some centuries back. Doctors would prescribe a comfort pillow for a sick person, putting an herbal mixture in their pillowcase to help them sleep. Comfort pillows were also used for the terminally ill (and it occurred to me that comfort pillows would certainly be a welcome addition to the sterile smelling hospital room, since many people relate how bad their dreams are while in the hospital). The fragrances of pure, natural herbs and flowers would boost the spirits, and the dreams, of the hospital or sick room patient.

Through my researching of old herbals I found that mothers in previous centuries would fill tiny pillows with dried catnip and put it in their baby's cribs to ease nightmares. Mugwort was also used for that purpose, and it is a traditional herb to use to ease nightmares in adults, as well. (Folklore also says that mugwort helps one remember dreams).

I wrote to Jeanne Rose, the author of numerous books on herbs, because I knew she had been making dream pillows in some of her workshops. She wrote back, sending me some of her recipes to try and telling me how much fun she has with dream herbs.

Over time I began to experiment with combinations of herbs myself, making up new mixes to evoke particular kinds of dreams. I began to give dream pillow workshops in 1985 and those evolved into my first *Dream Pillows & Potions* book. Also from the lectures and book, I began to make dream pillows to sell. I introduced several of my own dream blends and have received lots of letters and comments back from people telling me how much fun they've had using my little pillows (and lots of accounts of funny and colorful dreams).

My company, Long Creek Herbs, started wholesaling our dream pillows several years ago, making them available to even more shops around the country and the response to those has been very good.

I now frequently get requests for the recipes for more of my dream blends and I have debated whether I wanted to give away my "secrets." I simply decided that I can't possibly reach all of the outlets that could sell our pillows, and that sharing information only makes more business for us all.

I believe this ancient and amazing herbal craft, which has given me so much pleasure, should be demystified and incorporated into more people's lives. This will happen best when herb professionals share more openly their research, experience and results. More information, based on experience, will help raise the quality of dream pillows already being sold (as in the generic blends sold by a couple of companies, which are just fragrant herbs blended without any regard to the kinds of dreams they evoke - those are poor quality products and not worthy of being called dream blends, in my opinion.) In the same way that a broader public recognition of culinary herbs has opened up billions of dollars in businesses in the past 20 years, I believe an industry-wide revival of the use of dream pillows will produce both excellent new markets and benefits to us all.

Suggestion:

Dreams can be windows into creativity. Many writers and artists have told of their inspiration coming in a dream. While we sleep, our mind rests, kind of hums along in neutral. With the worries and distractions of the day, our creative nature can surface and wonderful ideas and projects can unfold. Use dream blends like the action blend, for releasing your creative ideas.

So, here, in this book, I give you my long guarded, "secret blends," my sources, my packaging solutions, all the things that have taken me years to learn, research, formulate and create, to make Dream Pillows a successful and profitable product. I hope you will have as much fun as I have with dream pillows, and that together, we can share with the herb-buying public our love for colorful, exciting and creative dreams, and make money, as well.

Happy dreams!

Chapter 1
Why Dream Pillows Work

Dream pillows are an ancient craft, based on how the fragrances of herbs and flowers affect memory. It's a form of aromatherapy and works like this:

You can be walking down the street and pass someone who is wearing a familiar cologne or perfume. Even if you don't see the person, the brief whiff of fragrance can instantly take your mind back in time to an event, a cherished moment or a former lover.

The fragrance of fresh bread baking, or of roses, can take you back in time in your mind. A bad aroma can evoke a memory from childhood, a good aroma can remind you of someone you hadn't thought of in many years. The point is, the aroma is the key to unlocking the memory in your mind.

Science tells us that our sense of smell accesses one of quickest routes to our memory, that our sense of smell is one of the first we develop as tiny babies. Our sense of smell is a strong and important sense that is vital to our existence.

People formerly used pine beds for the sick. This was back centuries ago, when beds weren't fancy to start with. A frame on the floor would be filled with fresh pine needles, packed down, smoothed out and covered. The belief was that the aroma of pine was healing.

If you've ever stretched out for a nap on a mat of pine needles under a pine tree deep in the forest, then you know how soothing the fragrance is. I've camped out many times in pine woods and always had delightful dreams, even though I didn't connect the aroma to the dreams.

A remnant of pine beds is the balsam fir pillows sold in gift stores in the northern parts of the U.S. I found balsam pillows in New York some years back, and found them recently when I visited a Shaker farm in that state. The instructions say that the fragrance of balsam fir is soothing and an aid in restful sleep. They

Suggestion:

When using balsam, pine or cedar needles, it is good to use heavy cloth, or use two layers. You don't want your customers complaining that they got stuck in the cheek during the night with a pine needle.

Suggestion:

Tell your customers about ways to see if they dream, like using a dream log. Mention this in workshops if you decide to give dream pillow workshops.

The more information your customers have about dream pillows, the more they will want to use them.

Also, you might mention to your customers that people who have lost their sense of smell, those who use heavy amounts of perfume or cologne, and those who are smokers, will not perceive the subtle fragrances in dream blends as well as others do and may not notice a change in their dreaming for 3 or 4 nights when using a dream pillow. Heavy smokers are often the ones who have little response to dream pillows. (If you are an ex-smoker, you will recall that abut 2 weeks after you quit smoking, you began to notice the aromas of food, flowers and other smells that you had been missing when you smoked.)

are a simple dream pillow, even though they are not sold as that. Balsam pillows come originally from Native Americans who, for centuries, have used the fragrant fir needles for peaceful sleep.

Dream pillows can be soothing for nightmares. They can help a person sleep, and they can be recreational. I like to look at some of my dream pillow blends as control knobs on my mind's television. Add a few herbs of this kind, a pinch of that for color, a bit of this for action, and I have a dream that is better, and more relaxing, than watching t.v.

What about people who don't dream?

Research shows that everyone dreams, it's just that some people forget their dreams immediately upon waking. If you want to increase your ability to remember your dreams, or to check to see if you do indeed dream, when you think you may not, there are several things you can do to facilitate that.

1 - You can use herbs that make dreams more colorful. Rosemary, roses, lavender and pine are a few of the herbs that add color (see herb list for more). Mugwort is said to help you remember your dreams and while this may be true, or it may be folklore, I continue to use mugwort in most dream blends and customers have reported back that they can remember their dreams after using my dream pillows.

2 - You can keep a dream log. Put a notebook and pencil next to the bed where you will find it when you get out of bed. Since the first 60 seconds after waking is the time your dream goes away, it's necessary to write it down immediately. You'll be groggy and not make much sense, but just write down a few words or a sentence. It will take several mornings before you get yourself in the habit of

writing, but over a few days, you will see that you actually were dreaming, after all. Starting a dream log before using your dream pillow will help you recognize how the dream pillow affects your dreaming.

3 - Try different dream blends on yourself. Try one for peaceful, restful sleep first. Use the pillow for several nights, then put it away and sleep a few nights without a dream pillow. Then try a more colorful dream blend for a week and see how your dreams are different.

There are other factors that can have an effect on how well the dream pillow works.

If your customer uses heavy perfume or cologne on a daily basis, her or his sense of smell may be a considerably diminished. It's what I call the "traveling salesman syndrome." As men get older they use more cologne because it makes them feel attractive (I notice this most among the men who are salesmen on the road). Also as we and they age, the sense of smell begins to lessen. The less they can smell, the more they feel the need to add more cologne. Combine the excessive cologne with a couple of packs of cigarettes every day and the wearer's nose is unlikely to any longer smell subtle smells. So, if your customer is a traveling salesman who uses lots of cologne and smokes, don't be surprised if he comes back and says, "I didn't notice any real changes in my dreaming."

Jay Leno, on The Tonight Show, *said recently, "Old Spice should be renamed and called, 'Grandpa's Substitute for a Shower in a Bottle,'" pointing up the fact that older men splash on too much cologne.*

Chapter 2
Herbs for Dream Pillows

Following is a list of herbs and their traditional uses for different kinds of dreams and dream blends. It is certainly not every herb that can be used for dreams. Out of the thousands of herbs and fragrant plants, there are certainly more. If you're going to make your own concoctions, different from the formulas listed in this book, I suggest that you try the blends out on yourself first before trying them on your customers.

Anise seed (*Pimpinella anisum*)

Curtin's *Healing Herbs of the Rio Grande* suggests that "the scent of anise seed inhaled, keeps men from dreaming and starting in their sleep, and causes them to rest well." I have no idea if this claim is true, but it's worth trying out on someone and getting them to give you the results. Try anise seed in a man's dream blend, something with other soothing herbs. I use about a teaspoon full, but Scott Cunningham, a writer I met several years ago, says in his *Cunningham's Encyclopedia of Magical Herbs*, "Fill a small pillowcase with anise seeds and sleep on it. This will insure that you have no nightmares."

Ash (*Fraxinus sp.*)

Cunningham, in the same book, above, lists ash leaves for dream pillows. "The leaves of the ash when placed beneath the pillow induce prophetic dreams." I have no experience using ash leaves, but they might be useful to try and I know of nothing harmful, nor any reasons not to use these leaves.

Balsam fir (*Abies balsamea*)

Fresh needles, or freshly-dried needles of the balsam fir are a delightful addition to the dream blend. Just a pillow filled with balsam fir needles is pleasant, or balsam with lavender, hops and roses, combine for a pleasantly relaxing dream pillow. I've found several places that still sell balsam fir pillows, which are actually dream pillows although they are not labeled that way. I saw them in upstate New York, at state park stores, and in southern New York at a Shaker gift shop. Specialty mail order catalogs carry them and fir pillows are a traditional tourist sales item.

Suggestion:
When formulating new dream blends, use the blend on yourself for several nights. Notice changes in your dreams and keep a log of the kinds of dreams you have.

Next, make up some pillows with your new blend and give a pillow to each of 3 or 4 friends who are willing to try your new mixture (and who are willing to report back to you on the kind of dreams they have had).

Look for reactions, both positive and negative. If your test dreamers report nightmares or headaches, check to see if you have looked carefully at the herbs you have used. Check to see that the material you used for the pillows was laundered without fragrance (the number one cause of headaches with dream pillows is not from the herbs, but from the dye and sizing in the cloth).

If you don't have any reports of unpleasantness, then focus on the kind and quality of dream your test dreamers have had. Not remembering color in a dream can usually be addressed by adding a bit more mint. (Some people do not dream in color, so not everyone will experience vivid color, but most people can be aware of more color with the addition of mint to the blend).

Basil *(Ocimum sp.)*

Generally not recommended for use in dream pillows. Sweet basil *(Ocimum basilicum)* is used in Eastern medicine, where it is called "tulsi," and is used to treat flu, emphysema and respiratory problems. However it contains methyl chavicol, which is moderately irritating to the skin (especially in concentrations of oils). Basil can cause headaches or what I describe as a vague "brown, groggy feeling" in the dream. It's best left out.

Bay *(Laurus nobilis)*

I believe that bay should never be used in a dream blend. According to my friend Billy Joe, bay was one of the herbs that caused the awful nightmares I had while visiting her house. Bay, like French marigold and tansy, seems to give the sleeper headaches upon awakening, and nightmares while sleeping.

Betony *(Betonica officinalis)*

In *Cunningham's Encyclopedia of Magical Herbs*, the author lists betony, also known as lousewort or bishopwort, as useful in dream pillows to keep away bad dreams and nightmares. I haven't tried betony in pillows, but you might like to experiment with some in a blend for yourself.

Calendula *(Calendula officinalis)*

This used to be called "Pot Marigold" although it is not related to the French marigolds. Calendula is usually thought of as a skin ailment herb (you'll find it in the pharmacy as "calendulated cream"). A bit of calendula petals or blossoms can add restfulness. Folklore says that calendula and sage together "makes dreams come true." That's the fun thing about folklore, it sounds great but may not be true. I doubt that calendula can make dreams come true but nevertheless I do use it in a few blends, to add a quieting aspect. And what are dreams, if not flights of fancy?

Catnip *(Nepeta cataria)*

A relaxing sleep herb. In centuries past, mothers would sometimes use catnip pillows in the baby crib to help their babies sleep more soundly. (We don't make any recommendation regarding that old practice, for while it might be effective for adults, there are lots of reasons why a baby might have restless sleep or cry in the night and few of the reasons would be cured by the use of catnip). Since catnip is

Suggestion:

The addition of hops is restful and relaxing in a dream blend. However, I have had customers write back with the warning that it shouldn't be used by recovering alcoholics. A few have written to tell me that they had dreams of bars and drinking. It makes sense because hops is a main ingredient in the brewing of beer and one of the primary fragrances in that beverage is a result of the hops oils. For the general population, however, hops acts as a soothing, restful ingredient in dream blends and I use it regularly.

Suggestion:

Calendula is easy to grow in your garden. It is an annual, so plant seed in early spring. The seedlings jump quickly to blooming size (about 14 inches tall). Harvest the opened flowers every day or two, laying them in a basket in your pantry to dry. When fully dry, store in air-tight bags, in a dark place.

If you do not clip the blossoms, or choose to let them go to seed, they will cease blooming and set seed, and in the region where I live, they die in mid-summer. Like some other annual herbs (sweet marjoram, for instance), the more you harvest, the more they produce and the longer they keep growing.

slightly sedative and relaxing, use this herb in blends for quiet, relaxing sleep.

Cedar (*Juniperus virginiana* or related species)

Cedar needles can be a nice addition to a woodsy dream blend. Use cedar sparingly, about 2 teaspoonsful to a pillow. Cedar berries, also can be used this way. Be sure, if using cedar or juniper, this has not been sprayed with chemical sprays. You may have junipers in your yard which have been sprayed to keep away red spider and bagworms. Don't use those for dream blends. The chemicals can really add unpleasantness to a dream (not to mention poison!)

Chamomile (*Matricaria chamomilla*)

Used for relaxation and pleasant dreams. However, for people who are allergic to ragweed, chamomile can sometimes cause a similar allergic reaction. If you are going to use it, be sure to tell your customers what is in the blend. Roman chamomile (*Anthemis nobilis* is also listed as *Chamaemelum nobile* in some sources), which is the creeping plant, is less useful than the well-known German tea herb. Use German chamomile sparingly (such as no more than a teaspoonful or two per pillow).

Cinnamon (*Cinnamomum zeylanicum*)

Cinnamon comes from a tropical evergreen tree with thick bark. You can grow cinnamon as a potted plant and the leaves will also have the pleasant, but fainter, fragrance of the mature tree. It is the bark that is harvested and ground into what we know as the spice, cinnamon. Studies by the fragrance industry in the past 5 years found that the smell of fresh-baked cinnamon rolls was the most powerful aphrodisiac fragrance for men they tried. So if you plan to make romantic dream blends and want to include something that gets the man's attention, include a small bit of cinnamon. Inexpensive cinnamon sticks will be *Cinnamomum cassia* (or simply listed as "Cassia") rather than *C. zeylanicum*. Why would that matter you may ask? Because the fragrance is much fainter, the cassia is a poorer quality substitute. The study was done with good quality *Cinnamomum zeylanicum*, the plant with the better fragrance. It is a bit more expensive, but you don't have to use as much. I recommend the better quality cinnamon as the most cost effective over all. Order from a reputable supplier and ask for their best quality cinnamon sticks.

Suggestion:
Chamomile is an easy annual herb to grow and if you grow it yourself, you can be sure it has not been sprayed with chemicals that could affect the dreaming. Plant chamomile seed in little pots or flats in early spring (about 3 weeks before your last frost date). When the weather is safe to put them outside, plant them about 14 inches apart. Plant at least a dozen or more plants if you plan to harvest the flowers for tea or dream pillows. Even though they produce thousands of flowers, the blossoms are small after they have been dried. Pick the flowers every other day, just as the blossoms begin to open from the bud stage. Dry them in a food dryer or in baskets in a warm, dark and airy place like in the pantry, on the top of a refrigerator where the air flows, in an attic or in a dark garage. Do not use the microwave to dry herbs! The microwave process vaporizes many of the tiny oil cells where the fragrance is located (you'll notice a pleasant aroma when you open the microwave door - that is the fragrance that was supposed to stay in the herb!).

Suggestion:
How do you know you are getting real cinnamon? You can't always be sure if you buy from discount sources. Good quality cinnamon is listed by oil content; 4% or 5% is a good quality oil content for cinnamon. Or, just smell it. Good quality cinnamon smells strong and full of fragrance.

Chamomile is correctly spelled Camomile *or* Chamomile, *according to the dictionary.*

Cinquefoil (*Potentilla canadensis* or *P. reptans*)

Known by several names, including Five Finger Grass, Crampweed, Five Fingers and others. Folklore abounds about cinquefoil in the Ozarks, as well as in the British Isles, where many of the ancestors of Ozarkers came from. It was said that the plant brings good luck, that by placing a sprig with seven leaflets (rare) under your pillow, you would dream of your future lover. Some sources say that a little bag of cinquefoil in the bed helps the sleeping person have restful sleep without nightmares. It's worth trying in a dream blend as I know of no cautions or reasons not to use this herb.

Cinquefoil is an easy to grow perennial and is attractive in the garden. It's native to much of the midwest and tolerates a wide variety of growing conditions. The plant blooms through the spring, then can be cut back for a second blooming.

Clary Sage (*Salvia sclarea*)

This salvia has a strong odor that is more useful for insect repellents or for fragrance in making soap. (A major producer of clary sage in the United States is the tobacco industry, which uses this herb as a flavoring ingredient in some smokeless tobacco blends). You might experiment with a very small amount of clary sage in your own dream blend, but be careful of using it for your customers. The fragrance of the plant, especially when combined with other aromas, may cause some pretty weird dreams.

Suggestion:
Clary sage is a biennial. Plant it in summer for blooming the following late spring to summer. At Longwood Gardens, near Philadelphia, clary sage is used as a bedding plant. They use beds of pink, white and purple clary sage side by side for a beautiful display.

Clove (*Syzygium aromaticum*)

Use cloves sparingly. I add 1 or 2 cloves to a romantic dream pillow. Mixed with roses and other herbs, the faint aroma of clove adds an exotic feeling to the dream.

Clover, red (*Trifolium pratense*)

In the language of flowers, clover hints at prosperity. In the dream blend it can be used to evoke pleasant dreams of pastoral settings, peacefulness and quiet. Use dried clover flowers or leaves, in small amounts (1-2 teaspoons). It might be fun to try combining red clover flowers and lavender, in equal portions, with just a tiny pinch of mint to see what kind of dreams that will evoke.

Suggestion:
Whole cloves are the more expensive product. For dream pillow purposes (and because you use such a small amount) a good substitute is to use clove stems. Clove stems are quite fragrant, but do not have the bud of the clove flower. If I'm cooking, I use whole cloves. For dream pillows, where fragrance, not flavor, is the consideration, I use clove stems. You save around $1-$2 a pound.
If you are going to buy cloves for your pillows, don't buy it in the tiny bottle at the grocery store. You can buy a pound from an herb supplier for nearly the same amount that you pay for 1/3 ounce at the grocery store!

Damiana (*Turnera diffusa var. aphrodisiaca*)

One friend who likes to experiment with dream pillows says that damiana adds a nice erotic kick to romantic and aphrodisiac blends. I've not used the herb, but you might research more about its effects and try a bit in a hotly romantic mixture. Try mixing it with roses, sweet woodruff, pine, mint and jasmine, with just a hint of rosemary and marjoram and if

your dreams aren't too torrid to write about, let me know the results!

Dill (*Anethum graveolens*)

Jeanne Rose has recommended dill seed or leaves for helping adults or children go to sleep. Just a pinch is enough, if using dill with other herbs. Or, a dill seed pillow, about 2 x 3 inches, is said to work for sleeplessness, too.

Hops (*Humulus Lupulus*)

The flowers have long been considered useful for encourage relaxing, pleasant dreams. There are several kinds of hops that are used in brewing beer and ale. The best kind for the dream blend is sweet hops (be sure to specify sweet hops when ordering your bulk herbs).

Suggestion:

Hops are easy to grow, but give them lots of room. In my grandmother's back yard, they took over the garden fence and climbed into the apple tree. It is an invasive plant, but if you have an arbor to let it run up on and can mow around the base of the plant, hops make an attractive vine. The part collected is the blossom.

Jasmine (*Jasminum officinale* or *J. odoratissimum*)

The fragrance of jasmine will almost make you dream when you are awake! The fragrance from a cup of hot jasmine tea is soothing and relaxing. The fresh flowers have such a lovely aroma that they are almost intoxicating. *Cunningham's Encyclopedia of Magical Herbs* lists dried jasmine flowers as good in dream pillows to induce sleep. I use jasmine flowers in some of my romantic and erotic mixtures because they combine well with some of the herbs in those blends and lend a lovely, slightly exotic feeling to the dream. Mixed with roses and lavender, hops and rosemary, the combination evokes some pretty interesting, loving and warm dreams.

Lavender (*Lavandula sp.*)

This favorite herb eases headaches, adds restfulness and soothes. Lavender can be used in quantity in a dream pillow. Just a pillow of plain lavender can be soothing, or a mix of half lavender and half mugwort is useful for that purpose, too. You just can't help but be soothed when picking lavender in your garden, and it works on your dreams, as well. One study recently demonstrated lavender fragrance can cause reduction of stress-related illnesses in elderly persons.

Suggestion:

Lavender requires well-drained soil (a raised bed in mid-America), some lime in the soil and full sun, meaning at least 8 hours a day. Given those requirements, lavender will perform well, giving you lots of fragrant lavender spikes. Harvest them when in full bloom, then cut the plant back a bit to encourage a second blooming late in the summer. In early spring, cut lavender back by half to encourage good blooming. Fertilize with compost and a dusting of lime.

Lemon Balm (*Melissa officinalis*)

It was lemon balm and lavender that caused my acquaintance with Hillary Clinton many years ago. I presented her with a lavender wand (another herb craft from centuries past) in which I had combined fresh lavender blossoms and lemon balm, at the dedication of the Heritage Herb Garden, a project I had researched and designed in 1985 and '86. She enjoyed the gift and a couple of years later ordered 49 more lavender wands to give as gifts to the governors' wives at the National Governors' Conference when she and Governor Clinton hosted the event in Little Rock in 1988. In aromatherapy, lemon balm is used as an antidepressant and for anxiety, insomnia and nervous tension. Lemon balm combines well with roses, lavender, thyme, hops and mint. A simple combination of lemon balm and lavender is relaxing, helpful to relieve headaches and stress.

Lemongrass (*Cymbopogon citratus*)

A native plant of tropical regions; you may recognize this herb as an ingredient in lemon-flavored teas and a seasoning herb in Oriental cooking. Use a small amount in dream blends to add some color to the dream, and to add a slightly exotic feeling. I like to use this with marjoram, because the marjoram seems to keep the dream soft with a safe feeling. (When using lemongrass, cut it in short pieces).

Lemon Verbena (*Aloysia triphylla*)

A native plant of Argentina and Chile, growing up to about 10 feet. Jeanne Rose showed me photos of the lemon verbena she has in her San Francisco garden that is a bit taller than average, and she sits under it with her afternoon tea! (If you haven't experienced the fragrance of lemon verbena, grow one in your garden. You'll want to just lay down and roll in the fragrant leaves!) I grow mine as a 2-3 ft. garden plant, pruning it often to obtain the delicious-smelling, lemony leaves. Cunningham claims that in folklore, lemon verbena was worn around the neck to keep a person from dreaming. I've found that a small amount, such as one leaf, when used with roses, lavender, hops and other dream herbs, can add a bit of lightness, sometimes encouraging those dreams of flying that many of us enjoy.

Life Everlasting (*Anaphalis sp.*)

A native plant in Europe, Asia and North America. I've not used this herb for dreams, although I gather

Suggestion:
Lemongrass is easy to grow in your garden. Give it full sun, next to the water faucet or other damp place. Harvest the leaves all summer long, then if you live in a region colder than Zone 8, dig the plant out of the garden, trim back the leaves to 12 inches tall and repot the plant for moving back inside for the winter. Next season, move the plant outside and plant back in the ground (it doesn't do well as a potted plant).

Suggestion:
In the pre-Civil War South, lemon verbena was used to scent the laundry. You can use it to scent linens by making up little pillows and placing them between sheets or towels.
Cool lemon verbena water in a washcloth is a soothing remedy to a hot afternoon. And lemon verbena tea is a refreshing beverage. Who knows, scented sheets may also give one good dreams!

it for dried arrangements in the fall. (Some of the plants in this family, known as "rabbit tobacco" and "pearly everlasting" are medicinal plants known to Native Americans, and have a wonderfully light aroma of butterscotch). From the following description, it sounds worthy of experimenting further.

"Perhaps the herb Everlasting, the fragrant immortelle of our autumn fields, has the most suggestive odour to me of all those that set me dreaming. I can hardly describe the strange thoughts and emotions that come to me as I inhale the aroma of the pale, dry, rustling flowers. A something it has of sepulchral spicery, as if it had been brought from the core of some great pyramid, where it had lain on the breast of a mummied Pharaoh. Something, too, of immortality in the sad, faint sweetness lingering so long in its lifeless petals. Yet this does not tell why it fills my eyes with tears and carries me in blissful thought to the banks of asphodel that borders the River of Life."

Oliver Wendell Holmes.

Linden (*Tilia x vulgaris*)

I gather the flowers from my father's linden tree to make a pleasant flavored tea, and for use in my dream pillows. In Europe, the flower tea is used as a relaxant and for indigestion. The ancient herb writer, Culpeper, said that the flowers are, "good cephalic and nervine." I find that linden flowers are relaxing and soothing and I use them with marjoram, lemon balm and lavender.

Marjoram, Sweet (*Origanum majorana*)

The word oregano comes from a Greek word meaning "joy of the mountains." The old sources list marjoram "for health," and used it as a soothing herb for nervousness and some say it smells a bit like balsam fir. I find that it adds a dimension of warmth, safety and comfort to dreams. In my romantic mixes, marjoram is one of the herbs I believe keeps the romantic mood light and pleasant instead of making the dreams about torrid love affairs.

Mimosa (*Acacia dealbata*)

In old herbals mimosa is listed as one of the herbs useful in prophetic dreaming. I think the dried flowers would be useful in dream pillows, especially ones where you are wanting to add an exotic undertone, such as dreams of far away places. I made a dream blend one year that I called, "South Seas Adventures." I had some mimosa flowers on hand

Suggestion:
Grow sweet marjoram as an annual for best results. The fragrance of the fresh plant is so very pleasant when harvesting and sometimes I clip a piece to put on the dashboard of my pickup when I travel, to make the vehicle smell fresh and herbal. Keep harvesting marjoram sprigs before the flowers bloom so that the plant will keep producing all season. (If you let it go to seed, the plant will die).

and included them in the mix. This is a flower that is worthy of experimenting with further. Try it with a tiny pinch of mint, mugwort, hops, a small dried orange peel, a clove, some frankincense or jasmine (but not both). I think this would make an interesting, if somewhat exotic, dream blend.

Mint *(Mentha sp.)*

Mint is an interesting herb because for me it can act like a tuning knob on a t.v. A pinch of mint adds brightness, color and clarity to the dream. Don't overuse mint by putting it into every blend, and don't use too much. A teaspoonful in a pillow is plenty, and a half teaspoonful might be better, depending upon what kind of dream you are creating. Peppermint, spearmint, or other mints can all be used. Some old sources claim that a tiny pillow filled with peppermint, placed under the sleeper's pillow will evoke prophetic dreams. (Maybe someone should gather up <u>all</u> of the herbs that were claimed by the ancients to evoke prophesy and put them into one single pillow, to test this old folklore! *See my "Prophecy" blend in the formulas section.)*

Mugwort *(Artemisia vulgaris)*

The common name comes from its former use, centuries ago, as a flavoring in beer. In folklore it is said that mugwort helps you remember your dreams. (My partner, who was tricked into using dream pillows by someone once because he didn't believe in them, swears it is true that the herb helps one remember dreams and claims mugwort warrants further study). True or not, mugwort is still a useful ingredient in dream blends and can be used at about the rate of 1 tablespoon per pillow (see formulas). Mugwort, is the only artemisia that should be used in dream pillows.

Mullein *(Verbascum thapsus)*

Often thought of today as an indigenous American plant, it is actually native to Asia and has naturalized across N. America. I love folklore, it hides little secrets and truths, but you often have to wade through lots of, well, folklore, to get to the useful material. For instance, mullein is said to instill courage; a few leaves placed in the shoe keeps you from catching cold. Wearing mullein while you are hiking protects you from wild animals. In the list of the folkloric uses of mullein, is this, "Stuffed into a small pillow...mullein guards against nightmares." (And to me, that hints at the plant's usefulness as a

---

Suggestion:

Never use essential oils or fragrance oils in dream blends. Essential oils (which are processed from plants) are much too concentrated and will overwhelm the other herbs, ruining the effect. Fragrance oils, which are chemical concoctions that imitate plant oils, break down in the air and can change radically in just a few days. Often made with a petroleum base, they can add feelings of emptiness, fear or haunting headaches when used in dream blends.

relaxing herb to avoid nightmares). I don't know of any other uses for this plant in the dream blend, but since it has ties to old medicinal uses for asthma, it might be worth trying as a nightmare preventive. I don't know of any reasons not to use mullein in a pillow, and if you have good luck using it, write and let me know.

Onion *(Allium sp.)*

An old Ozarks superstition claims that putting an onion under the pillow will produce prophetic dreams. Or if you wanted to make a decision, you would scratch a word referring to your options or choices on the side of each of 3 onions, put them all in the dark and whichever onion sprouts first, gives you the right decision. Well, personally, I don't think onions are worthy of putting in a dream mix, but if you feel strongly about it, then there's no reason not to try. Just don't be surprised if your customers aren't excited about the dreams they have of standing over a hot skillet of fried potatoes and onions!

Orris root *(Iris germanica, var. florentina)*

Orris root is a perfumey fixative for potpourri, with a fragrance that is much too strong for even that, in my opinion. (The smell of orris root reminds me of the time I got caught in an elevator full of perfume sales people, all trying on their samples). Remember that potpourri is not suitable as a dream blend and neither should be substituted for the other. Orris is not recommended for dream use.

Passion flower *(Passiflora incarnata)*

Suggestion:
If you plan to grow your own passion vine, be aware that it can be invasive. My parents grew passion vine on the fence at the edge of the yard where the lawn mower kept the many sprouts from the roots in check. Other than the shallow, underground runners that spring up with new plants, passion vine is easy to grow and attractive on the trellis or fence.

I harvest our lovely native passion flowers at the edge of the woods on the hill above our farm. You'll find passion vine herb (the leaves and flowers) listed as a sedative in reliable herb references. We offer it in capsule form in combination with valerian, wood betony and other herbs, as a relaxing supplement that helps you fall asleep. The passion part of the name comes from a story about the flower looking like a cross, thus, the "passion" of Christ. When using the leaves or flowers in experimental blends, remember that it relaxes rather than excites passion. Therefore it wouldn't be a good ingredient for a romantic blend unless you intend to put the lovers to sleep.

Patchouli (*Pogostemon cablin*)

Patchouli is one of those herbs the you either love or hate. In Malaysia it is used to treat headaches, nausea and other complaints (internally). It might be worth trying a tiny piece of leaf in a dream blend, especially one like a romantic mix, where you use roses, lavender and lemon balm. Use it sparingly and try it on yourself and your friends before you attempt to market this mix. (Some people have a strong, adverse reaction to patchouli, possibly because it seemed like the whole world reeked of the oil back in the '60s, while others think of it as a wonderfully nostalgic fragrance.)

Suggestion:
Patchouli is relatively easy to grow as an annual herb. Give it full to part sun (a little less sun than basil requires, generally), water often and you can produce quite a bit of patchouli during the growing season. The more you clip, the more it produces.
Some patchouli plants have more fragrance than others, when dry, so you may want to keep starts of your patchouli plant over winter, to be sure you have one with good fragrance.

Rose leaves (*Rosa eglanteria*)

If you grow this ancient scented-leaf rose, it is wonderful to use in your dream blends. The leaves can add a spicy bit of romance to a dream blend or, used with just hops or rose flowers, rose leaves will help create a pleasantly-relaxing blend. Try it in an adventure mixture, also. (Why not some romance mixed with adventure?)
Experiment using *Rosa eglanteria* leaves with lavender, hops, rosemary and a bit of chamomile; add just a pinch of mint, maybe a clove bud and just the slightest pinch of chili seasoning. I predict you may have passionate dreams!

Suggestion:
The best roses to grow for dream pillow use are the old-fashioned shrub roses. Many have not changed in centuries, have not been hybridized or tinkered with. The pink and red flowered ones generally have the best fragrance. Inquire at your nearest botanical garden if they are growing old-rose varieties and decide which ones have the best fragrance before you buy plants from a nursery. Several companies specialize in old rose varieties, including the Antique Rose Emporium in Texas. You can have a blooming-sized plant in just a season or two and it will supply you with lots and lots of rose petals for dream pillows, vinegars, rose syrups and more.

Rose petals (*Rosa sp.*)

Add roses to create a feeling of loving thoughts and warmth in dreams. Combine rose petals and buds with lavender and hops for a simple, pleasant dreams pillow, or use roses in combinations that have more complex combinations of herbs. The aroma of roses can add love, even eroticism to a dream, depending upon what other herbs are used. Be sure, if you are using rose petals you gather yourself, that they have not been sprayed with insecticides. The roses you buy for dream pillows should be "food-grade" roses, without any chemicals, oils or insecticides.

Suggestion:
Gather roses for drying during mid-morning, after the dew has dried but before the hot sun evaporates some of the fragrance oils.

Suggestion:
Clip the long sprigs of rosemary and hang them in an airy but moderately dark place (like a garage, attic or pantry) to dry. You can also clip lots of little rosemary branches and put them in a basket on top of the refrigerator or freezer where it is warm, dark and has good airflow from the appliance's motor. When completely dried, store in air tight container in the pantry.

Suggestion:
You can harvest sassafras limbs in winter or summer. Cut only the green, new growth. It's tender and you can use pruners to snip up the wood into 1/4 inch pieces. Let it dry for several days. (This is very important: make sure the wood is completely air-dried. Otherwise, when you store it in bags it could mould, and possibly give your dream pillow customers allergic reactions or cause unpleasant dreams).

Rosemary (*Rosmarinus officinalis*)

In folklore, rosemary is used to insure sleep and keep away bad dreams. To me that means that it is a soothing herb and I use it in my restful sleep mixtures. Rosemary works well with a bit of lavender, roses, mugwort and hops, for a relaxing night's sleep without notable dreaming.

Sage (*Salvia officinalis*)

Generally not recommended in dream mixes or aromatherapy. It can cause headaches and a vague sick feeling in a dream pillow.

Sassafras (*Sassafras albidum*)

I find that sassafras adds a slight spicy fragrance when used in small amounts. I prefer to use the wood of the limbs, rather then the leaves or roots, because it has a fresh, lemony-spice fragrance. I combine sassafras wood, cedar and pine needles, orange peel, a bit of clove, a little frankincense and a good amount of mugwort, for a mix that gives woodsy, pleasant dreams.

Sweet Woodruff (*Asperula odorata*)

This is another herb found in folklore that was believed to protect one from nightmares. It is a soothing herb and is useful in small amounts in the peaceful sleep pillow, usually with lavender and roses. Combined with other more exotic fragrances (like a clove, jasmine, etc.) sweet woodruff can add a mildly-exotic feeling to the dream.

Tansy (*Tanacetum vulgare*)

Not recommended for dream blends. Use tansy in your moth-repelling blends instead and give the moths nightmares!

Thyme (*Thymus sp.*)

Thyme has been used in dream pillows for centuries to insure restful sleep and a lack of nightmares. I've never used it by itself, preferring to combine it with roses, hops and lavender or rosemary. Folklore says that wearing thyme allows you to see fairies, so you might make little pillows to wear on a string around your neck and see if fairies appear; wear it on moonlight nights and watch very carefully to see if fairies come out to play; sleep with the pillow to see if you dream of fairies, too.

Valerian (*Valeriana officinalis*)

In aromatherapy valerian is used for insomnia, migraines and tension. A little bit is probably useful in a relaxing dream blend, but it should be used *very sparingly*. It smells strong, kind of a combination of gym socks and a goat. Really, that's the description people in my workshops have given when I pass around valerian capsules. Unless you are sure of your customer, you should probably use some other herb for relaxing in the dream blend, or use only a tiny amount. But, if you have a sleepless, nervous customer who is used to sleeping with an old goat wearing dirty gym socks, this may be just the herb to use!

Suggestion:
Valerian is an easy plant to grow in the garden and you can harvest some of the flowers for experimenting with in dream pillows. However, it is the ground root that has the pungent odor, and is the part of the herb that has been used as a relaxant and sleep aid for centuries.

Vervain (*Verbena officinalis*)

Vervain has lots of ties to magic and you can explore those in many old herbals if you're interested. One bit I thought funny relates to remaining chaste for long periods. You are instructed to rise before the morning sun on the first day of the new moon, gather vervain, and press out the juice and drink it down. (This is no small feat, vervain doesn't have a bounty of juices to start with!). According to ancient folklore, you'll lose all desire for sex for seven years. Hidden in the long list of folkloric uses of vervain is the hint that it keeps away nightmares and gives relaxing sleep. I've not used this plant, but you might try it sometime when you are having troubled sleep. It is a useful plant for many purposes and is worth adding to your store of relaxing herbs.

Vetiver (*Vetiveria zizanioides*)

The roots have been used for fragrance for soaps, perfumes and incense in Eastern traditions for generations. I grew vetiver one year. It looks like a clump of pampas grass, but isn't hardy north of Zone 8 or 9. In Sri Lanka the oil from this plant is known as the "oil of tranquility." The roots are more subtle in aroma than the oil, but unless you have grown up with the fragrance, it may seem a bit strange and too cloying. (Friends have told me about the curtains made of vetiver roots that add a pleasant scent to the room, but it may be a scent that has to be smelled in its native environment). I don't care for the fragrance, but if you like it, there's no reason not to experiment with small pieces of the roots. I recommend small amounts and caution when blending vetiver with other aromas, only because it may overwhelm the other fragrances.

Herb friends in Louisiana told me they grow vetiver as a hedge, just like some gardeners use pampas grass to divide one space in the lawn from another. They dig up the vetiver clumps in the fall, divide them and pull out great handfuls of roots in the process, then replant as many clumps as they want for the coming year. They then wash the roots in water, hang them to air dry, then finish the drying in the food dehydrator. When the roots are crisp, they break them up in bags and seal them for use later. They sell theirs in tiny bundles an inch in diameter and 6 inches long, tied with a ribbon, at craft fairs.

Suggestion:
Although violets are easy to grow, they are another herb that can be invasive if given the wrong location. My friend, Bertha Reppert of The Rosemary House in Mechanicsburg, PA, uses her Parma violets (a fragrant, old-fashioned violet) as a ground cover under her larger shrubs. The violets spill out onto the lawn in the shade of the house, and in the spring Bertha picks baskets of violets to use for all kinds of crafts. The lawn dotted with purple violets is a beautiful sight.

Violets (*Viola sp.*)

In folklore violets were believed to be a powerful love stimulant and arouser of lust. Violets have a sweet fragrance, but Dr. Arthur O. Tucker at Delaware State University, says that violets also have a chemical that numbs your sense of smell, so you can't detect the smell beyond the first sniff. (The essential oil concentrates the oil and does not seem to have the numbing effect like the fresh flowers have). But, I don't ever recommend using oils in dream blends as they are too unpredictable and hard to control. Generally speaking I don't use violets in dream blends, but some old sources include them and there's no other reason I can think of not to use violets and they do add nice color to the blend.

The rose looks fair, but fairer we it deem
For that sweet odour which doth in it live.

Shakespeare
Sonnets

About Insects & Your Herb Products:

It's extremely important that you keep bugs out of your herb products. Many health food stores have grain moths flying around inside and you can be sure if you buy products from them, you'll have grain moths soon, as well.

It's a constant battle to keep bugs out of your shop and work area. The main culprits are these:
- Indian Meal Moth & Mediterranean Flour Moth
- Warehouse Beetle *(Trogoderms variabile)*
- Cigarette or Tobacco Beetle *(Lasioderma serricorne)*

Most chemical sprays that will kill these pests are not safe to use around food and herbs. Additionally, chemical sprays should never be used on or around dream pillow herbs. That makes it difficult to control the insects that like to live and thrive in plant parts. There are some things you can do to effectively control, and even eliminate the pests.

1 - Bag everything brought in from outdoors! Any material you gather and dry from your own garden should be bagged and left in the freezer at 0° for 5-7 days, before storing it in your shop or work storage area.

2 - Immediately inspect all packages you receive from any bulk herb source. The best sources use a process of releasing carbon dioxide (the stuff you breathe out after taking in oxygen) into "tents" or storage rooms they have built for that purpose. The carbon dioxide stays in the air-tight area for 3 days, which kills any insects, eggs or larvae. But that doesn't mean that the material won't get reinfected in their warehouse. Check your shipments. If you find bugs, seal them up, get them out of your area and call the supplier immediately to tell them the shipment was infected.

3 - Be careful what you store in your work area. Don't store grain, like wheat, corn, oats, in any form (especially not ears of corn, shocks of wheat, etc.) in your facility. If you're going to keep leftover products from year to year, keep them in a freezer. My recommendation is to dump those unsold products at the end of the season because bugs love this stuff and you wind up having problems later. Peppers, (including dried peppers, pepper strings, pepper pods on wreaths and dried, ground peppers) work like magnets to grain moths. If you are going to store these in your shop during the summer months when the moths are most active, then keep them in the freezer in the off season. The freezer is also a good way to kill moths/eggs/larvae that you find in a product before you decide what to do with it.

Suggestion:
(If you are in doubt about what insect you have, your local University Extension Office can often help, or call the IPM Co. and ask if they will help you identify your sample).

Suggestion:
Even garlic braids can house the Indian Meal Moth. Refresh your stock every year. If you feel you must hold over garlic braids from the previous year, freeze them a few times. It's not good for the garlic, but then, after hanging for a year, there's nothing left of food value, anyway!

4 - Use pheromone traps (*see address for the Integrated Pest Management, or IPM company in the resources*). Pheromone traps are little cardboard things that hang, or sit, on a shelf. Each trap is coated with sticky-trap compound on the inside and there is a little bait cap, as well. The moths are drawn to the attractant, they crawl inside and get stuck. Replace the traps every 3-6 months and use one for about every 10 x 10 ft. area, or check the manufacturers' instructions.

Suggestion:
If you plan on selling your products at craft and herb fairs, keep your herb products in zipper bags until right before the doors open, if possible. Keeping the stock in plastic tubs or cardboard boxes doesn't completely keep the grain moths out but it does slow them down slightly. Their favorite place to lay eggs is along the edges of boxes or jar lids. Simply covering products in your booth the night before with a cloth isn't reliable, either. Grain moths are experts in looking for tiny crevices and going underneath things.

The best solution is to keep everything in zip bags as long as possible. Then when you return home to your shop, make sure everything gets bagged and run through the freezer before putting it back in your work area or shop space. It's one of the costs of taking your products to an environment where other people may not be as careful as you are about insects.

5 - **Keep your stock in plastic zip bags.** For dream pillows (and we follow this method for all of our dried herb products), keep the packaged pillows in larger, 2 gallon size zipper plastic bags. If the stock has been in your warehouse for more than 2 months, cycle it through a freezer (yes, it does take lots of zip bags).

We run all of our products and bulk herbs through a freezer during the summer months. Every week the freezer is emptied of bags and new ones go in. This helps to insure that our products do not get buggy.

6 - **Be especially careful at craft fairs.** One of the most common ways to get bugs into your storage area (other than bringing them in from a supplier, or bringing them in on the herbs you harvest yourself), is from booths at craft and herb fairs. I've walked around on the night before an herb festival and looked at the products displayed. Almost without exception, you will see several grain moths flying around. (They are most active at night, so late in the evening is a good time to see them). Herb festivals must be like a giant buffet for these insects, and they spend the night cavorting, laying eggs and spreading around their brood. Then, if you don't sell all of your products, you take the bugs home with you where they multiply like crazy.

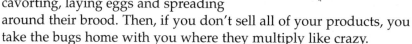

The solution is, and granted it takes some effort, to put everything in air-tight bags when you bring it home from the show and leave it in the freezer for about 5 days.

7 - **Tobacco and warehouse beetles are harder to control.** There are pheromone traps for them and they must be checked often to see if the traps are working. These insects fly, but aren't as obvious as the grain moths. You may find them in mint, lavender, lemon balm and other herbs, where they will turn the contents into a fine dust within days. The beetles themselves crawl slowly and are about the size of a mouse dropping. They hide under packages, between shelves and on the underneath sides of equipment.

8 - **Keeping your floor and work area swept and clean**, vacuuming the shelves and washing them every few months and cycling everything through the freezer are the best controls. If the problem

gets too bad for these methods, you are faced with sealing everything up in double zipper bags and setting off insect bombs or calling an exterminator. But be careful that the chemicals do not get into the herbs and products as this can ruin the effectiveness of your dream pillows by causing your customers to have allergies, headaches, nightmares, etc. (Even then, after using the insect bombs, you will still need to run the products and bulk herbs through the freezer to make sure there were not eggs hidden in the bottom of the bags that the poisons didn't reach).

Suggestion:
Train yourself, or your employees, to sweep up the work space every day. Keep the work area clean; put away all herb and plant materials. If you are working on a dream pillow project and will continue it the following day, don't leave things out. Take the few minutes of extra time to put everything away at the end of the day. Leaving the materials out over-night is an open invitation to insect problems in that product batch. Preventing the problem is much easier (and cheaper) than solving it later.

Keeping the bugs out of your products is always better than having to get rid of them once they arrive.

Chapter 3
Things to Consider Before Making Pillows

"A Bag to Smell unto, or to Cause one to Sleep: Take dried rose leaves, keep them close in a glasse which will keep them sweet, then take powder of Mints, powder of Cloves in a grosse powder. Put the same to the Rose leaves, then put all together in a bag, and take that to bed with you, and it will cause you to sleep, and it is good to smell unto at other times."
from Ram's Little Dodoen, 1606.

Suggestion:

Quality hand-made products are in very high demand. However, don't be tempted to cut corners by using up your old scraps of material if you plan to go after the market for quality-priced dream pillows.

Choose a fabric that works well with the name of your dream pillow, and that matches the color of your label. Hand-made doesn't have to look rustic and the better the quality, the more you can charge.

Before you begin, here some suggestions that might be helpful for making your dream pillows. All are based upon our experience and mistakes we've made, or little things we didn't think of in the beginning.

• If you are making several dream blends, choose one fabric for each. The easier it is for your customers to keep the blends visually and mentally separate, the more likely they are to buy.

• Coordinate your cloth with the labels on the dream pillow package. While it is tempting to buy bargain fabric in short yardage, you only confuse your customers by having a "potpourri of fabrics" all displayed together. This can hurt your sales. One suggestion a marketing expert gave me years ago was "Assume that your customers are fourth graders and you have less than 3 seconds per product to get their attention and sell your message." It sounds insulting to your customers, but it works. You've got the time it takes for a customer to cast a sweeping glance over your assembled products to get their attention. You must get them to pick up the package and read further. Having a single cloth design for each pillow blend simply insures that the customer gets the message that this product is distinctive.

• Take your tax number when you shop for fabric (you must do this if buying for resale). Most fabric stores like crafters shopping in their store and will save you the taxes, possibly even offer you a small discount, when you present your resale number. Ask the manager before you go to the checkout line as there is often a short form to fill out, which the store then keeps on file.

• Some of the nifty, rolling cloth cutters work great for cutting

out multiples of anything. I don't use one when I cut out dream pillows, but Connie, who does most of the sewing for our pillows, uses one and her work is much neater than mine.

- Cut your fabric and sew up all but one side (the open side is the one you will fill later) of your pillows before washing the material.

- ALWAYS wash your dream pillow material after cutting up and sewing the pillow (but before filling it). Why? The dyes and sizing in cloth will adversely affect your customers' dreams. We were having customers write back to tell us they were having overly-vivid dreams and headaches upon waking, after using one particular dream pillow. We tracked down the problem to some heavily-dyed material that I had not thought necessary to wash. Always, *always* wash your dream pillow material in a low phosphate detergent without perfumes and dry it without fabric softener before you fill the dream pillow.

- It's faster to cut out several yards of material at one time and stack these until you are ready to sew. I cut the material, sew up all but the fill side, wash, dry (and iron if necessary), then put the pillow blanks into 2 gallon zipper bags until I'm ready to fill and sew them shut.

- Don't store these dream pillow "blanks" next to other herbs or fragrances. Put them in zipper bags and zip them closed.

- Keep track of the time it takes you to make dream pillows, from mixing the blend to sewing and packaging. Add in the cost of materials and divide by the number of finished pillows. That should give you the per item cost and give you an idea of how to price the finished pillow. You should plan on adding on about 50¢ each for your talent, ideas and other incidentals (insurance, facility, etc.). Then double the price, or even triple it for the mark up. (See more details about pricing on page 54).

- It's not necessary to know much about sewing in order to make dream pillows. I have little skill in sewing, beyond having taken an upholstery class in college, and sewing patches on my own clothes growing up (thanks to my mother, who worked and said, "If you're going to tear up your clothes playing, you might as well know how to repair them.") I still use my grandmother's 1918 treadle Singer sewing machine, that she converted to electric about 1950. It's simple and rugged and I can crank out several dozen pillows per hour.

- One of the most cost-effective ways to produce dream pillows if you are going to hire help is by piece work. Paying someone by the hour is sometimes the most expensive way to produce a product. The speed at which one person works may be vastly different from the speed of another, and it can cause you nightmares in trying to keep your costs in line. To avoid the uncertainty, consider farming out the sewing and filling portion of your dream pillow operation (if

Suggestion:

Spend a few extra dollars for a heavy duty stapler and avoid using sharp staple points which scratch bags, labels and customers. We've had the best luck with a stapler that looks like a big pair of pliers, the Stanley Bostitch model B8 Plier Stapler. *It outlasts electric staplers and the desk-top models, and is easy to use. You can get it at office supply stores.*

you plan to make hundreds or thousands, for example). Establish a per-item price that you know you can afford, yet is still attractive to someone working at home. A price of around 20-25¢ per pillow is reasonable, if the person cuts, sews, washes, irons and fills the pillows. You can do this on contract labor, instead of having an employee on the payroll, which saves you some tax money (check with the tax laws to be sure you set this up right). Consider a retired person who likes the idea of being able to make extra money by working at home.

•One caution regarding piece work: You have less control of your product. Make sure the worker understands these important points: (1) No smoking around the cloth, filler or dream blends; (2) Do not leave the herb blends nor the sewn pillows where kitchen/cooking odors will penetrate, or where flying moths from the worker's pantry could infest your product. (3) If the worker has little children, make sure he or she understands that there are to be no sticky little fingers playing with the pillows and no cat sleeping in the pillow pile, (something that is very attractive to cats!) If the worker is not diligent about all of those concerns, you could have an inferior product, and customers who complain and don't come back to buy your other products.

Steps for Making the pillow (see pattern)

The pattern that I have included (on page 30) is for an approximately 4 x 5 inch pillow, which will fit into a 6 x 6 inch plastic zip bag (see sources for suggestions and sizes).

1 - Lay out the cloth and measure off the piece. For this example, you are going to cut out only one piece, but if you were in production, you would cut quantities at this point.

2 - Turn the material wrong side out (the side with the least printing), fold it over in the middle and sew up 2 sides (the fold makes the third). You have one open side left and that remains unfinished for now.

3 - Wash the unfinished pillow in the washer, on cold or warm setting, with a non-perfumed detergent. Dry on low heat without fabric softener and remove from the dryer immediately. Iron if necessary if the cloth isn't wrinkle-proof (this is important to having a professional-looking product; don't go to all this work then have a wrinkled pillow to sell).

The Steps to Filling the Pillow

1 - Take a small handful of Fiberfil (which is available at fabric and discount stores) and place it in the bottom of the pillow. Push it out so that it isn't just a lump. It should fill up about half the cloth pillow and spread somewhat into the corners.

2 - Place 1 or 2 tablespoons of dream blend in the center of the pillow (on top of the Fiberfil). Add enough Fiberfil to almost fill the pillow. You want the pillow to be filled and pleasant, but not puffed up like a melon. Fold over the cloth at the top (the place where you are filling the pillow). Sew the fold securely from end to end. Your pillow is now completed and ready for packaging.

To package your pillow, place inside a bag any printed instructions you want to include, place the pillow inside, zip the bag closed and attach the header tag with staples. (Insert on page 42).

Your pillow is now ready for sale. *(See more about packaging in that section in Chapter 5, page 41.*

The pillow

The pillow, packaged and ready to sell

If you haven't done production work before, you will quickly see that you can use your time most effectively if you make several dozen at a time, first cutting them all, then sewing, then washing together, lining them up and filling with Fiberfil, then adding the mix, more Fiberfil and finally finishing them up in one sitting at the sewing machine. You'll be surprised how many you can turn out while watching television, if you like to work that way.

Dream Pillow Pattern

One-half of the dream pillow cloth is shown due to limitation of the page size. Double the length for the correct size. Because of the fold at the bottom, it isn't necessary to sew that side. Dotted lines show the sewing line. The finished pillow will be approximately 4 inches x 5 inches.

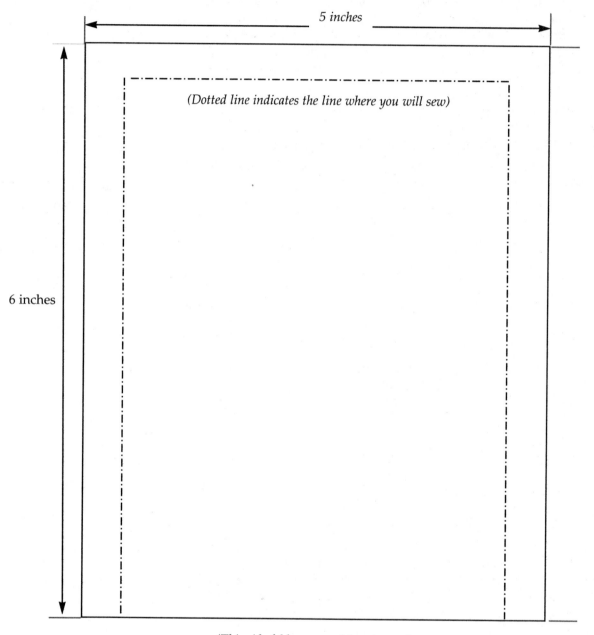

(Dotted line indicates the line where you will sew)

5 inches

6 inches

(This side folds over and is not sewn)

Chapter 4
Jim's Secret Formulas

This is the both the most difficult chapter for me to write and the most exciting, simply because it has taken me years of experimenting to come up with these formulas and I have guarded them even from my employees up to now. My philosophy has changed and I have come to realize that sharing my formulas will actually increase my business, rather than decrease the market.

I've tried all kinds of herb combinations and slept on mixtures to see how they work. I've kept records in my letter file of customer's comments on various blends. I've used my friends to try out formulas and have used trial and error to see what works and what doesn't.

You can use these formulas as they are, or you can use them as foundation formulas upon which to build other blends of your own. I've included tips throughout the book; things which occur to me to mention to you as you read about making money with dream pillows. The tips have come, often, from mistakes I've made, or from customer's suggestions. If you heed the tips, they save you from making the same mistakes.

You will recognize that I am overly sensitive about smells, such as insisting that people who smoke not make my dream pillows, that no one smoke nor eat food around dream pillows, and that dream pillows never be left in the open air at a craft fair. I've watched other crafters make those mistakes and noted how their mistakes have hurt their sales, either by customers telling them directly, or by customers who have come to my booth and mentioned the other crafters' mistakes.

Use the plant list in Chapter 2, which includes the descriptions of what kind of dreams they evoke, to create your own blends. You'll notice that there are more blends and mixtures woven throughout the plant descriptions in the form of suggested combinations, so be sure to read and use those, too.

The following formula came about because of Mike, our friend and press operator who prints our books. He had read my Dream Pillows & Potions *book and said, "Well, those are fine, but I'd like something more exciting than a 'Pleasant Pillow,' and I don't need a 'Romantic Dreams' or 'Relaxation' pillow."*

I asked him what kind of dreams he would rather have and his reply was, "Oh, something with action; I'd like boats, horses, mountains, color, excitement. A dream that is entertaining."

"I can do that," I said, and got to work on the following blend. The first time I used this blend on myself, I dreamed I was a pirate. (I've never been on a ship, by the way, nor sailed on the ocean) The ship was shiny black, freshly-painted wood set upon a deep blue sea under a vivid blue sky. It was a wonderful dream and this has become my favorite dream blend for my own use. I look upon it as like reading a good book and it is especially useful for encouraging creativity.

Suggestion:

Leather shops and leather crafters seldom have any use for their leather shavings and little scraps. Tell them what you are looking for and ask to buy a pound or two. You can easily use the slivers cut from the edges of leather work, or the "dots" left from cutting the holes in belts. Leather crafters use a shaver, much like an electric plane that wood crafters use. The shaver shaves off very thin layers of leather to smooth out thick leather when using it for various leather items. That works just fine for your dream blend. If you're going to make lots of this dream mix, then find the cheapest source. (If the leather person is intrigued enough by what you are using the scraps for, he or she will trade you the shavings in exchange for a dream pillow. However, since the leather person works with the scent of leather all day, he or she will probably respond to another blend of dream pillow that does not contain leather).

Action Dream Blend

1/4 cup chopped pine needles
1/2 cup mugwort
4 dried French marigold blossoms, petals only
1 small (about 1 inch long) stick cinnamon, crushed
4 whole cloves or clove stems
1 cup rose petals
1/2 cup lavender
3 tablespoons chopped leather trimmings (from leather shop, or cut from new, inexpensive leather gloves). Leather is tanned with tannin, from oak bark, and the scent is important for this mix. Don't use old gloves which will have lots of "foreign" smells on them.

Mix ingredients together and leave in a closed plastic zip bag or air tight, lidded, plastic container, for 3 or 4 days. To use, take out 2 tablespoons of the blend and place it in a 3 x 5 inch cotton muslin bag, or put that amount into your pillow on top of the Fiberfil and finish as described in the pillow-making instructions section.

Remembering Dreams & Encouraging Sleep Blend

1 cup plain mugwort leaves in pillow.

Be sure to use only Mugwort *(Artemisia vulgaris)* from a reliable source. If you grow it yourself, make very sure that you aren't harvesting Motherwort *(Leonurus cardiaca)*, an herb that looks similar, which many people can't distinguish, visually from *A. vulgaris*.

Sensual Dreams

3 tablespoons rosemary
1 tablespoon mint
4 tablespoons rose petals
3 whole cloves or clove stems

Mix well, keep in zipper bag away from light for 3 or 4 days for the fragrances to blend together. Then the mixture is ready to put in your dream pillow. For larger amounts, substitute cups or pounds.

Pleasant Dreams #1

This is our best-selling blend, year after year. It's what I call a "generic" blend because a pleasant dream is unremarkable, just quiet sleep and little pieces of dreams floating by. But lots of people like this and we have received good comments back from customers. If you want a good-selling, all around blend, this is it.

1 cup mugwort
1/2 cup rose petals
1/3 cup chamomile
1/3 cup lavender
1/3 cup catnip
2 tablespoons mint

Mix all ingredients and set aside for one week, in a zipper bag. Use 2 tablespoons per dream pillow, in the center of Fiberfil. *(These instructions are the same for the following Pleasant blends)*

Suggestion:

Make your formulas in small amounts, such as in the amounts listed here, to try out the blend. Then when you are ready for larger production, just substitute "pound" in the recipes. Often I list formulas as "parts" and you can use pound, cup or bucketful for the part and the ratio of the herbs used, once well mixed, is still correct. All ingredients listed in the mixtures are for dry herbs.

Pleasant Dreams #2

1 cup roses
1 cup catnip
1/4 cup mugwort
1/4 cup hops
1 tablespoon sweet marjoram
1/2 tablespoon chopped lemon verbena stems or leaves

Pleasant Dreams #3

1 cup roses
1 cup lavender
1 cup catnip
1 cup mugwort
1 cup hops
1/4 cup marjoram
1 tablespoon linden flowers

(continued...)

Suggestion:
To try out a dream blend, sleep with it for 3 to 5 nights in a row to see what effect the herbs have. Then adjust the mixture and try it on your dreams again.

(Pleasant #3, continued)

1 tablespoon lemon verbena leaves

Mix well and place in zipper bag, away from light, for about 3 days. To use, place 1-2 tablespoons in dream pillow. I've found that one heaping tablespoon is enough in the standard 4 x 5 inch pillow, with Fiberfil for fluff.

Generic Dream Blend

This is the "one-size fits all" blend that a national wholesale herb supplier sells, except that they stretch it with cellulose, (also known as finely ground corn cobs!). You can do better by using Fiberfil, which makes a softer pillow. By making this one yourself rather than buying the herb company's blend, you can save money and make more profit for yourself. I have included the formula here so you will know what is available, and what your competition may be selling. It's not a good dream mix. However, this mixture smells good on the shelf, like a weak potpourri (good dream blends are more subtle with a fainter scent simply because you are going to be inhaling the herbs all night). Experiment with this blend on yourself before deciding to use it on your customers.

1 cup rosebuds or rose petals
1 cup mugwort
1/2 cup peppermint (that's a lot of peppermint! I'd reduce it to 1 tablespoon)
1/4 cup lemon verbena (I would reduce this to 1/2 tablespoon herb, chopped)
1/4 cup chamomile

Relaxing Dreams #1

This is my blend for people who are having nightmares, or are prone to fitful sleep, sleeplessness, etc.

1/2 cup lavender
1/2 cup mugwort
1/2 cup sweet hops

Mix all ingredients together and place in a plastic zip bag for 24 hours. Put 2 tablespoons of the blend in the standard dream pillow, surrounded by Fiberfil. Or, put about 1/2 cup of mix in a cotton muslin drawstring bag, tie closed and place in your pillowcase.

Relaxing Dreams #2

1/2 cup mugwort
1/2 cup lavender

Mix as above.

Relaxing Dreams #3

1 cup hops
1 cup mugwort
1/4 cup marjoram

Relaxing Dreams #4

1 cup roses
1/2 cup rosemary
1/2 cup lavender
1/2 cup hops

There are always some doubters in the crowd when I give my dream pillow workshops. I like to cut an orange in half and pass it around; I open up a fresh package of Juicy Fruit gum and pass that around. Then I ask for comments from people as they smell the fragrances. A response to the fragrance of oranges that I hear often is, "I always think of Christmas when I smell oranges" or, "Juicy Fruit reminds me of my grandfather." The speed at which memories are brought out, just from passing around those 2 fragrant objects demonstrates how easily the fragrances in dream pillows work on our mind as we sleep.

Romantic Mixes

I've included several different blends here. I find that my customers are the best sources for ideas for products. To that end, a young couple walked up to our booth one day and looked over the dream pillows. The young fellow said with a grin, "Gee, you've got romantic pillows and action pillows. Ever consider combining the action mix and the romantic mix?" Actually I hadn't thought of that, but it bears some experimenting. Here are my two most romantic blends.

Romantic Dreams #1

1 cup roses
1 cup rosemary
1/2 cup lavender
1 lemon verbena leaf, crushed
1 teaspoon mint
4 whole cloves
1 small piece cinnamon, 1 inch long, broken up
Optional: 1 tablespoon dried violets

Mix, store for 4 days in zipper bag. Use 2 heaping tablespoons per pillow.

Romantic Dreams #2
(the Erotic Blend)

A customer wrote back to tell us that, "Not only does this romantic dream pillow work, but I can't possibly bring myself to tell you how well it worked!"

    3 cups roses
    2 cups rosemary
    1 cup lavender
    1 tablespoon mint
    pinch (less than 1/8 tsp.) ground cloves
even smaller pinch of commercial chili seasoning
2 lemon verbena leaves
1 piece cinnamon bark, 1 inch long, broken into pieces
Optional: pinch of damiana, if available
Optional: leather shavings. Be careful though, this adds a wilder, more uninhibited dimension to the pillow!

Mix well, put aside in a zipper bag and let the fragrances blend for about a week. Then it's ready to use. For the standard pillow, a heaping tablespoon per pillow is enough.

Suggestion:
If you are going to use roses for dream blends and don't have a good source for food-grade, fragrant roses, then consider growing your own. I grow several old rose varieties, shrub roses that have not been hybridized. They produce masses of heavenly-fragrant roses in a short time. I gather them every day in baskets and dry them in the food dryer, then bag them in zipper bags. Shrub roses are easy to grow, require no spraying of insecticides and offer you the best quality rose petals you will find anywhere.

Exotic Dreams #1

Customers using this blend report dreams of flying, lots of color, happy feelings and exotic, colorful places. It's a really good blend and you can have fun finding a better name to describe the kinds of dreams it evokes.

    1 cup hops
    1 cup calendula petals
    1 cup roses
    1/2 cup catnip
    1/2 marjoram
    1/4 cup lemon verbena
    1/4 cup jasmine flowers
    1/4 cup lavender
    2 tablespoons mint

Exotic Dreams #2

This one gives a lighter feeling dream, with more flying; a favorite of folks who like Star Trek and science fiction. It has movement, yet feels safe and pleasant.

    2 cups roses
    4 cups calendula petals

(continued...)

4 cups rosemary
1 cup lemongrass, cut in short pieces
1 cup sweet woodruff
1/2 cup mugwort
1 tablespoon mint
1 tablespoon marjoram
1 teaspoon fennel seed
1 lemon geranium leaf (such as Mable Grey)
1 piece of cinnamon bark, about 1/2 inch long, broken

Mix and store in zipper bag for several days. Use heaping tablespoon per dream pillow.

Holiday Blend

This is a pleasantly colorful blend that we use in our Holiday Dreams Pillows, popular at Christmas because of the many seasonal associations it evokes. (The part of our brain where we process smells is very near that portion where long-term memory is stored, so aromas experienced in childhood are usually good in dream pillows).

3/4 cup mugwort
1/2 cup roses
1/4 cup catnip
1/8 cup pine needles, cut small
1/8 cup cedar needles, cut small
2 tablespoons sassafras wood, cut in small pieces (see plant descriptions, p. 20, for part used)
2 small pieces orange peel
2 small pieces lemon peel
1 tablespoon lemongrass, cut small
1 tablespoon rosemary
1/8 teaspoon frankincense
1/8 teaspoon myrrh
8 whole cloves
1 piece stick cinnamon, about 1 inch long, broken into pieces

Suggestion:
Gather evergreens in chilly weather by harvesting short limbs. Bring them back home and cut them up with pruners on newspapers or into a large container, in a warm, comfortable place. Sometimes I do this job in front of the television at night. The fragrance makes the house smell wonderful. Of course you have to vacuum afterward to pick up any stray pieces. Still, it has become a wonderful winter ritual that I enjoy.

Deep Woods Blend

An outdoorsy mix that is great for dreams of camping and hikes in the woods.

1 cup mugwort
1 cup roses
1 cup catnip
1/2 cup rosemary
1/2 cup pine needles, cut small
1/2 cup cedar needles, crushed or cut small

(continued...)

1/4 cup balsam fir needles, cut fine
1/4 cup sassafras wood (see plant list for description)
1/4 cup lemon balm
1 tablespoon lemongrass
2 whole cloves or clove stems
Optional: 1 tablespoon lemon verbena leaves
Optional: 2 tablespoons leather shavings (which will add more action and a more aggressive dream)

Mix and place in zipper bag for 1 week. To use, place 1 heaping tablespoon per pillow.

Traveler's Comfort Dream Blend

A customer told me how helpful a dream pillow is to her when she travels. "My first night in a hotel, I can't sleep. I think it's my mind adjusting to the smells in the linens, the room, and so on. I take a favorite dream pillow from home, keeping it in a plastic bag when I travel. As soon as I get my bags unpacked, I place my dream pillow inside the pillowcase. I have much better sleep with a familiar smell."

1 cup mugwort
1 cup roses
1/2 cup lavender
1/2 cup marjoram
1 tablespoon passion flower, leaves or petals

Mix and store in zipper bag. Use 2 tablespoons per pillow. Use the pillow at home from time to time, storing in a zip bag between uses. Take it when you travel and use it in hotel rooms, or even guest rooms in friend's homes. The familiar fragrance will be calming and help you sleep. Just remember to remove the pillow before the maid cleans the hotel room!

Help With Fitful Sleep Mix

(For those having troubled sleep)

1/2 cup catnip, placed in muslin drawstring bag. Place it in the pillowcase. This is an old method for calming a baby that cries in the night (although we don't recommend you use it for that purpose; babies can cry for very good reasons and not all are necessarily remedied by catnip pillows).

South Seas Dreams

This is a somewhat exotic but peaceful dream blend. I like to call it my "Vacation in a pillow blend."

1 cup roses
1 cup mugwort
1/2 cup hops
1/4 cup lemon verbena
1 tablespoon lemongrass
1 tablespoon jasmine flowers
1 tablespoon chopped mimosa flowers
1 tablespoon mint
2 whole cloves
1 small piece orange peel
Optional: 2 tablespoons marjoram

Suggestion:
You can buy dried orange peel, but it is cheaper to make them yourself, and the fragrance of what you dry will be vastly superior to what you buy.
Buy several oranges at once and use them for juice, feed them to the kids, etc. Save the peelings and lay them out in flat baskets or on newspapers. If you have a furnace that blows hot air from a vent, put the peels where the air blows over them several times a day. When the peelings are crisp and break easily, they are ready to bag up in zip bags.

Mix, store in zip bag and leave for 4-5 days. One heaping tablespoonful per pillow is enough.

Prophesy Mix

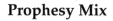

I thought it would be interesting to combine several of the folkloric herbs that the ancients claimed would give insight into the mysteries of the world. I believe that it takes a lifetime of learning about life to gain insight, but some cultures in the past believed it was simply a matter or combining the right herbs and placing them in the pillow. Try this one just for fun. If you have a bout of insight into the mysteries of the universe, please write and share them with me!

1 cup thyme
1 cup vervain
1 cup rose leaves (*R. eglanteria*)
or fragrant rose petals
1 cup peppermint
1 cup mugwort
1/2 cup marjoram
1/2 cup mimosa flowers
1/4 cup sweet woodruff

Mix, let set in zipper bag for 1 week. Use 2 tablespoons per pillow or muslin bag.

Convalescent Blend

An old herbal recommends these herbs be used for the person who is recovering from illness. The recipe (I've added the amounts to use as none were given) calls for lilac blossoms. Lilac is my "most favorite" fragrance in flowers, and I can easily see why they would be included to lift the spirits of someone in recovery.

Suggestion:
Gather lilac blossoms while they are in bloom and dry them by hanging them upside down in a warm but somewhat dark place, like in your garage, pantry, attic, etc. The color dries well and you may be surprised how much fragrance stays in the withered blossoms.

1/2 cup lavender
1/4 cup heliotrope
1/4 cup lilac blossoms

Mix together and place in zipper bag for 3 days. Use 2 tablespoons per pillow or muslin bag.

In 1830, Macnish, the author of The Philosophy of Sleep *wrote that, "A pillow of hops sometimes succeeds in inducing sleep, when other means fails. Such as was the case of his late majesty, George III, who, by this contrivance, was relieved from that protracted wakefulness under which he laboured for so long a time."*

Good packaging is important!

Chapter 5
Packaging and Sources

Packaging can make or break you. How the product looks to the customer is very important. You have to get the customer's attention, get your message across about what the product is and sell them on the idea of investigating further, all in less than 3 seconds. A good package will entice the customer to read further, to pick up the package and possibly to ask a question. A badly packaged product fails to get the customer's attention and they walk on to the next booth.

While traveling with my lectures and workshops, I have watched crafters selling their dream pillows. One example comes to mind of a lady in another state who had a booth at an herb conference. Her products were well-made, with nice materials and workmanship, but she was short on ideas for packaging.

Her dream pillows were not wrapped at all. Her display consisted of a little flat basket, filled with 4 x 6 inch pillows. Each had an inch-sized piece of notebook paper (lined, even!), pinned to the pillow with a straight pin. On it in ink pen she had written the blend and the price. The basket contained romantic blend pillows, some restful pillows and others. Of course the fragrances all quickly spread throughout the pillows, so by the time the customer got the pillow home, there was no real difference in aroma from one pillow to another.

The use of notebook paper and a straight pin made it look, not homey and hand-made (like she probably assumed) but unprofessional, rushed and unplanned. Her labeling looked like she had decided to make dream pillows for the conference about 3 days prior, and at midnight on the night before the conference, had said, "Oh, my, I don't have any price labels. Johnny, do you still have that old bunch of notebook paper you're not using?"

Another example I recall was from a music and new age gift store. They had pillows that were about 2 x 3 inches, made of deep blue and gold brocade, trimmed with tiny gold tassels with gold braid on the edges and really well-crafted. The price tag was one of those gummed, white Dennison labels and it read, "$14.95." There was no distinction of what kind of dreams one might have, and since

Suggestion:

It is absolutely necessary to protect the smell of your dream pillows by packaging or wrapping them. Otherwise, you might as well sweep up the floor sweepings of all the herbs left on your production room floor at the end of the day and call that a "blend." If you are going to go to the effort to produce a unique blend, then you need to be sure that no other fragrances creep in, and that the aromas you have put in your pillow stay there. And, too, the package is some insurance against insects that could damage your products.

Suggestion:

Perceived value is a term that describes how a customer perceives your product. If you make a good product and package it poorly, you reduce the value of the product in your customer's eyes. Use professional-looking packaging, good header tags and neat price stickers. Avoid notebook paper, straight pins, plastic wrap and other items that make your product look cheap. "Cheap" doesn't sell. Neat and attractive packaging sells products.

Suggestion:

Place your staples high enough on the tag so that they do not puncture your zip bag. The more airtight the zip bag stays, the more protection you have for your product.

(continues on pg 45)

This page is ready to photocopy. Make copies on plain bond paper, cut them in half and fold to fit inside your Dream Pillow package. Add your business name at the bottom if you wish. Use white-out or white masking tape to cover up this wording.

Instructions for Using Your Dream Pillow

Dream Pillows are based on how fragrance effects memory. If your mind flashes back to a pleasant memory when you encounter a fragrance (like roses reminding you of your grandmother, or a perfume or cologne reminding you of a boy- or girlfriend), then Dream Pillows will likely work for you. Dream Pillows can last for years and they're lots of fun to use. You may want to use the pillow for a week or two, then put it away in a clean plastic zipper bag for a week or two, then use it again. Used in this way, Dream Pillows can give you many wonderful dreams and can last for years.

Note: Dream Pillows are very different from potpourri. You won't detect a strong fragrance through the package; the subtle aroma of the herbs is released as your head moves around on the pillow while you sleep.

If you are allergic to plants, or if you sneeze or have headaches when using your Dream Pillow, discontinue use. Dream Pillows contain only natural, dried herbs and plants, no oils or other fragrance. Happy Dreaming!

Instructions for Using Your Dream Pillow

Dream Pillows are based on how fragrance effects memory. If your mind flashes back to a pleasant memory when you encounter a fragrance (like roses reminding you of your grandmother, or a perfume or cologne reminding you of a boy- or girlfriend), then Dream Pillows will likely work for you. Dream Pillows can last for years and they're lots of fun to use. You may want to use the pillow for a week or two, then put it away in a clean plastic zipper bag for a week or two, then use it again. Used in this way, Dream Pillows can give you many wonderful dreams and can last for years.

Note: Dream Pillows are very different from potpourri. You won't detect a strong fragrance through the package; the subtle aroma of the herbs is released as your head moves around on the pillow while you sleep.

If you are allergic to plants, or if you sneeze or have headaches when using your Dream Pillow, discontinue use. Dream Pillows contain only natural, dried herbs and plants, no oils or other fragrance. Happy Dreaming!

Header tag master. Add your shop name on the back (top section). On the front, add the name of your Dream Pillow (such as Romantic, Action, etc.). Add that lettering by use of a computer or typesetter. Then take the page to a Kinko's or other copy store and have the page photocopied on colored CARDSTOCK. Cut the pages in half, trim off any excess and fold your header tag in half. Attach to the zipper bag with a stapler.

Note: When all of your wording is in place, this will be a "Camera-ready" page. You can then take it to a print shop where the printer can turn your page into as many labels as you want. Kinko's and other quick-copy stores are the cheapest method if you want 25 or 50 header tags. But if you are ready for 200, 500 or more, the print shop method is best and will give you the best price. *Paul's Printing (417) 272-3507; FAX: (417) 272-3707 offers quality printing, which is fast, efficient and will ship your order anywhere.*

Only one header tag is illustrated here to save you time. You need only do the lettering or typesetting on one example, have it photocopied and use a glue stick to make 2 on this page. Then you are ready to have the page photocopied, then cut the completed page in half, trim, fold and you have inexpensive header tags ready for attaching to the top of your Dream Pillow package.

(*Your shop or business name here*)
address

They are lots of fun to use, and, yes, Dream Pillows do work!

Dream Pillows are a centuries-old craft, dating back to 16th century Europe where people used fragrant herbs to stop nightmares, ease restlessness or to help evoke pleasant dreams. This Dream Pillow is formulated for a specific kind of dream. Dream Pillows are based on how the mind responds to fragrance. (If familiar smells, like the smell of bread baking, or roses, reminds you of a pleasant memory, then Dream Pillows will probably work for you).

Fold

(Put Name of your Dream Pillow Here)
Dream Pillow
A Blend of Natural Herbs
to Promote (kind of dreams) Dreams

Dream Pillow is to be tucked inside your pillowcase
to encourage pleasant dreams

Suggestions for making your header tag

To make your header tag, get a clip art book (they are copyright-free; you can use their artwork without getting sued). The other alternative is to produce artwork, or hire someone to produce art work for your header. However, do not simply photocopy something out of a book you have seen somewhere. Copyright laws are specific and you are likely to get caught and sued; you don't need that. Simply pay the $5 for a clip art book and clip something out. Clip art is also available on CD-ROM for your computer and is easy to learn to use.

Attach your clip art in the space provided on the header tag to customize your header tag, by cutting it to approximate size and putting it in place with a glue stick. (If you don't know glue sticks, then you need to get acquainted with how handy they are. For about 89¢, you can buy a glue stick that is useful for all kinds of office and paste up art work.) Add your company name on the space provided by using the glue stick again. Make sure it is lined up straight with the bottom of the header tag.

Now, with your clip art in place, make one photocopy so that you will have a second copy of the clip art. Cut and glue stick it in place on the second half of the header example to make 2 on a page.

Suggestion: Don't use a typewriter to put your business name on the bottom of your header tag. Use a computer. If you don't have one, find someone who does. Or, for $5 per hour you can use IBM or Mac computers at any Kinko's store. Or, walk in to a business that does typesetting and ask them to make a two or three line original of your business name. (You can make as many copies as you need from that, cutting and gluing it in place; don't cut up your original). Typesetting will probably cost you $5 or $7.

With everything in place, take your original (the other side of this page with your business name and clip art pasted into place), to your best copy store. I prefer Kinko's Copies because they are in every college town, give great service, have an excellent assortment of papers to choose from and you are free to use their paper cutters, glue sticks, scissors, etc. on the work tables they provide for their customers.

You will want your header tag printed on CARD STOCK, which is a heavyweight paper different from the paper you will use for your instruction insert sheet. (For an example of card stock, look at the cover on this book). Card stock will cost between 12¢ and 24¢ per sheet, depending upon where you go, and the paper costs in your area. (Keep in mind, you will be cutting the sheet in half and getting 2 header tags per sheet of paper).

Office Depot, BizMart and similar office supply stores also offer printing, often letting you do your own copy work. That can save you money if you are familiar with how to make your page look its best on the machine, but if you are after quality, speed and friendly service, I recommend Kinko's over any other copy service.

CARD STOCK will be available in several colors. Choose a color that will make your dream pillow look its best. I use bright red card stock to go with my romantic dream pillows which are sewn up in red and white material.

Remember, once you have put your label together to run off at the quick copy store, it is camera-ready, and can be taken to a printer for volume pricing.

If you are printing 10-50 header tags, the cheapest way, and certainly the fastest, is the quick-copy store. But if you are ready for 200 or more header tags, the most cost effective method is to use the print shop. The printer will photograph your original, then print it on the paper you choose, with the ink color you want. This is the best quality printing, and the cheapest for volume printing. Still, the quick-copy method is a good place to <u>begin</u> because you can get 1 or 50 labels printed to try out on your packages with minimal cost.

the pillows were not packaged in any way, they would have taken on the smells of other products in the glass display case. I checked back a couple of times to see if the dream pillows were selling. Over time the prices were repeatedly dropped until finally they disappeared.

In both examples the product did not sell well, not because the product wasn't good, but because the packaging and display was poorly done.

Option #1 - Zip bags with header tag. We often get compliments on our packaging and those comments are always gratifying. I've spent several years trying different methods of packaging, and have found that the most cost-effective method is the first one I will describe here, with a bag and header tag. The advantages are that you can package a lot of pillows in a fairly short time; the materials look professional, yet are inexpensive, and you have room to increase production using my method.

We package all of our dream pillows in 6 x 6 inch zipper bags (the A60602 bag from Action Bags). We started with sandwich zip bags (Ziploc pleated sandwich bags, 6 1/2 in. x 5 7/8 in.). They were nearly the right size, although we had to make a little fold in the bag so that it fit the pillow better, which cut down on the customer's perceived value. In the beginning that worked fairly well as we had not found a better bag and we could go to the grocery store and buy several boxes of bags at a time (which, by the way, is not the least expensive way to buy bags unless you only plan to make 50 dream pillows to sell).

Let's say that your pillow is made and securely inside the plastic zip bag by this time. You next want to be sure to include a small instruction sheet (we use one half of an 8 1/2 in. x 11 in. piece of paper, folded in half again). I've included one on page 42, ready for you to photocopy. Place the instruction sheet behind the pillow, folded in such a way that the instructions can be read by the customer. Zip the bag closed and you are ready to attach the header tag.

A header tag is simply a folded, printed card, with a label on one fold and your company name on the other. Header tags are the least expensive kind of labeling, the most durable and versatile, for this product.

Suggestion:

If you are going to display your dream pillow packages in baskets, consider not putting several kinds in one basket. When a customer walks up and sees several of anything lumped together in a basket, it says to them, "close-out," "old merchandise." (Don't you always look at the discount shopping cart at the discount store where everything is all thrown together and the price tags have marks through them?) Your customers have been trained by the discount stores to expect mark-downs and close-outs all dumped together. Even though your products are new and spiffy, the customer will see them as old items you need to get rid of by the way you have displayed them. The all-in-one-basket method makes the product look bad.

Instead, neatly arrange each blend in its own basket. Sales will be better and you will also be able to see at a glance which pillow is selling best for you.

Suggestion: *To determine the cost of your packaging, add the cost of the label, the instruction insert, the plastic bag, the staple and the labor. You will probably be spending around 20-25¢ per pillow for packaging.*

Suggestion:

Always put the price sticker on the bottom or reverse side of a product, never written on the label on the front. Writing on your label looks like you're not serious about your business. Putting a neatly-printed price sticker on the reverse side encourages your customer to pick the package up, turn it over and read further about the product.

The longer you keep the product in the customer's hands, the more likely they are to buy the product.

Suggestion:
Keep your pillows, materials and bulk dream blends away from cigarette smoke. Customers who are sensitive to cigarette smoke (and most former smokers fall into this category) will detect the smoke residue in the blend and not have a good reaction to the dream.

Suggestion:
Be cautious about displaying your dream pillows in a booth that has a smoker next door. The smoke will likely collect on your products and the smoke smell will remain. Those who do not smoke will smell the cigarette residue and put the pillow back down.

Suggestion:
Give your dream blends more creative names than the ones I have provided here. Check your Thesaurus for more descriptive words. Know who your customers are and make products (and names) that encourage them to want to buy the product.

The header tag is slipped down over the zipper part of the zip bag and stapled in place.

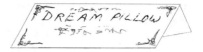

Header tag, folded and ready to use

You can use a hole punch and put a hole at the top of the header tag if you wish, or consider using clear plastic hang tabs.

Hang tabs are sticky on one end, come several to a sheet and are easily applied to the top of the header tag. This makes a neater package (and eliminates punching a hole); you can then hang the dream pillow package on a pegboard if you wish. Hang tabs can be ordered from Action Bag.

Option #2 - Boxed pillows. If you are going to sell your dream pillows in up-scale shows and shops, then you might consider the boxed dream pillow. The packaging is a bit more expensive for this, but it also raises the perceived value of the product and you can charge more. A 6 1/8 in. x 4 1/2 in. transparent note card box is an excellent size for dream pillows. You simply lay the instruction sheet in the bottom of the box, place the pillow on top and put on

the transparent lid. Tie a piece of ribbon around the box, place a custom-printed dream pillow label on the lid and a price sticker on the bottom, and your product is completed.

Here are some factors that make this a more expensive package, and something to consider when deciding on your packaging:

1 - The transparent boxes cost about 40¢ each, including shipping them to your shop.

2 - Printed stickers for the top will cost you about 10¢ each

3 - Ribbon adds a small price, as well.

However, if you are going for the up-scale market, the package looks really good and they can be assembled quickly.

Option #3: Use of a muslin drawstring bag and Dream Pillow folder. We offer printed dream folders that make it easy to market a small dream pillow. To assemble the product, simply put 2 tablespoons dream blend into a 3 x 5 inch cotton muslin drawstring bag, tie it closed and insert into the attractive gift folder. Tie a short piece of ribbon at the top and bottom, in the holes provided, and your dream pillow gift folder is ready to sell. These work especially well for Christmas or Valentine gift shows and fairs.

Advantages of this packaging option include the speed which you can assemble the product, and the low cost.

The disadvantage to this option would be that the product is not sealed in a plastic bag or container. However, you can store the filled dream folders in zipper bags and simply take them out for display at craft and herb shows.

Option #4: Dream-O-Gram®. One of our most exciting products using dream pillows is the Dream-O-Gram®. It is made especially for the customer who wants a unique and thoughtful gift. It consists of a large (8 1/4 in. x 6 1/2 in x 3/4 in) book folder that holds a completed dream pillow in a zip bag with header tag. The Dream-O-Gram® folder is printed in antique brown with dream pillow history, instructions for use and a place for signing a personal message inside. Gift boxes for the Dream-O-Gram are available, as well. The customer can choose the kind of dream pillow they want, and give you the address of the person who is to receive the Dream-O-Gram®, The box is closed and sealed, addressed and sent to the recipient. We've had wonderful letters back from people who received their Dream-O-Gram® gifts.

Advantages to this option include the perceived value for the customer and the added service (the customer makes the choice but you do the work of shipping the gift at the appropriate time). This option is for the more sophisticated customer. Suggested price for the complete Dream-O-Gram® would be $14.95-$16.95 + postage.

The disadvantage is the little bit of additional time involved in putting the pillow in the folder and closing up the mailer, then addressing the package and sending confirmation to the customer.

The Dream-O-Gram® folder, smaller Dream Folder and muslin drawstring bags can be ordered from Long Creek Herbs, (listed in the Sources section). Dream-O-Gram® folders and the Dream Folders are copyrighted and may not be copied, but we offer them for sale for wholesale shops at a reasonable price. Custom printing is available if you are interested in special versions of these packages in large quantity for your shop.

(For our wholesale customers who buy our dream pillows or bulk herbs, we offer a sample of the Dream-O-Gram® and Dream Pillow folders for $3, including postage).

Our Dream-O-Gram® folder is an easy way to increase the perceived value of your dream pillow.

Packaging Sources

Suggestion:
If you don't find the packaging source you need here, check with a trade organization. Most professional herb associations offer a search or referral service to their members. It's another way that being a member of a trade organization pays you back!

The following companies will sell to you provided you have a resale tax number and business card or company letterhead. Minimum orders are listed where that information is known. Most companies will ship a sample of a bag or item for you to see before you order, usually with only a charge for postage (call and ask about information about samples). All will ship a catalog to you upon request.

Note card box, 6 1/4 in. x 4 1/4 in. x 1 1/8 in., item #602x404x102 from:

Transparent Container Co.

345 N. Western Ave.
Chicago, IL 60612
(312) 666-4413; FAX 312-666-3163

Call and request a catalog. Their minimum order is $200. They also stock round transparent boxes and several other useful packaging products.

Zip bags, hang tabs, paper bags for shop, tissue paper, shredded packing material, cotton drawstring bags, custom-printed labels, display strips for hang tabs, etc. The dream pillow zip bag we use is the A60602. Call Action and ask for a sample:

Action Bag
501 N. Edgewood Ave.
Wood Dale, IL 60191
(800) 824-2247
Minimum order $50.

Tissue paper, ribbon, bow machines, candy-type gift boxes, and some really good natural-looking craft paper custom labels:

Mid-Atlantic Packaging Co.
14 Star Lifter Ave.
Dover, DE 19901
(800) 284-1332
Minimum order $25.

Decorative tin boxes, reship cartons, custom-printed metal boxes, gift ideas for holiday sales:

US Can
8901 Yellow Brick Rd.
Baltimore, MD 21237
(410) 686-6363.

Suggestion:
It isn't necessary to do so, but companies usually appreciate knowing how you heard about them. You are welcome to mention the author and name of this book as the source, because we have done businesses with nearly all of the businesses listed here and gladly recommend them.

Boxes, (some perfect for dream pillows) available in small quantities or large, with labels or without. Order their catalog, then ask for sample of any boxes you are interested in:

Mod-Pac Corp.
1801 Elmwood Ave.
Buffalo, NY 14207
(716) 873-0640

Bulk herbs for making dream pillows, dream pillow blends in bul, muslin drawstring bags, dream pillow supplies including gift folders, books, dream pillow kits and ready-made dream pillows, both wholesale and retail:

Long Creek Herbs (the author's company)
P.O. Box 127
Blue Eye, MO 65611
Phone or FAX orders: (417) 779-5450
$50 minimum first order. Visa & Mastercard, company check, phone and fax orders accepted.

Herbs in bulk (1 lb. to hundreds of lbs.)

Frontier Herbs
PO Box 299
Norway, IA 52318
(800) 669-3275

$20 minimum order once you are an established customer. While this is a nice company to deal with, you must pay a fee (they are a co-op and you must be approved as a customer. I've been told by their customer service department that they turn down customers who are not herb-related. Just be aware that they have to approve you and you have to pay a $40 co-op fee to "join." Then there is a small fee added to every order to maintain their co-op). Still, they have good prices and quality, ship the same day as you order and give a small end-of-year rebate. If you will be buying lots of herbs, consider buying from Frontier.

Herbs in bulk
San Francisco Herb Co.
250 14th St.
San Francisco, CA 94103
(800) 227-4530

There's nothing to "join" with SF Herb Co, but they do have larger minimum orders. Call and ask for their catalog.

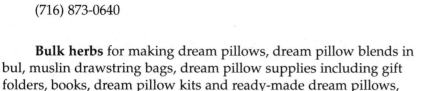

Pest management (how to control those flying grain moths in your shop) by use of pheromone traps, sticky traps, etc.

Great Lakes IPM, Inc.
10220 Church Rd., NE
Vestaburg, MI 48891
(517) 268-5693
(800) 235-0285

Inexpensive Pantry Pest Traps art available in many hardware stores, but if you can't find them there, call:

Consep, Inc.
213 S. W. Columbia
Bend, OR 97702
(800) 367-8727

They sell The Pantry Pest Trap in boxes of two that are easy to use in your shop.

Suggestion:
Attend an herb conference. Trade conferences are the best places to find sources for products and services. If the company or product is not represented at the conference, visit with others in the business and ask them for suggestions. Even though it appears to the small business person that attending a conference is too costly, you may find that it will actually save you money. The cost of attending a conference is around $350, travel and lodging, plus meals can round off your expenses to around $900-$1,000. (Of course you can find ways to economize, like room-sharing, driving instead of flying, etc.) I have found that the ideas, contacts, new customers and fresh perspectives more than pay for the trip. And, it's a great way to stay ahead of your competition! See the listing for Professional Organizations and contact them for information about the conferences and trade shows.

Chapter 6
Marketing Your Dream Pillows with More Resources

My philosophy about marketing is based on these points:

1 - Always sell a good product that you believe in and can honestly recommend.

2 - Be as professional and honest about the product as possible. Don't make claims that you can't back up and don't promise something you can't deliver.

3 - Don't discount your stock, don't sell seconds or damaged packages, it only hurts the sales of your good products and makes it look like you are about to go out of business.

4 - Be consistent, meaning create a good product and stick with it. The crafters who show up every year at a craft show with a different product line are the ones who are struggling to get by. Do like Orville Reddenbacher said, "Do one thing and do it well," (and the customers will come to you).

5 - Deal with the customer in a way that will encourage them to come back again and again because they were happy with your products <u>and</u> service.

6 - Offer the customer something they can't get elsewhere, either in the uniqueness of your product, or in the way you treat them.

7 - Organize and display your products so that you can maximize the sale, meaning, have peripheral products that relate to your product. For instance, when the customer buys your dream pillows, they also buy my *Dream Pillows and Potions*, book that you have displayed nearby, along with any other related products you offer. Each related product your customer buys increases the per-visit sale to your shop or booth. Every time the customer buys more per visit, your overall profits for the year will increase.

8 - Listen to your customers, to both their questions and their comments. It is from my customers that some of my best products have come.

Orville Reddenbacher said, "Do one thing and do it well."

My grandmother said, "Do what you really love and everything else will take care of itself."

Suggestion:

If you are just starting out selling herb products or crafts, you may be tempted to put your items out on consignment. Don't! It seldom works, unless you have a very dedicated friend who is pushing your products in the store.

If you do decide, against all advice, to do consignment sales, then consider following these guidelines to avoid problems:

(1) Keep good paperwork; list every item, price, percent you pay the store and date you leave the product. Take the list with you every time you service the account.

(2) Make sure your products are being displayed well; specifically, don't let the store owner dump them all in one basket like they are "close-out" items.

(3) Refresh the products often (every other week is ideal). Take out damaged or soiled product packages and replace them with clean, fresh ones.

(4) Give the store a written statement at the end of each month and don't let them put you off on your payment. They have collected the money, and it is yours to collect from them, as well.

(5) If at all possible, avoid doing consignment with relatives and friends. They may mean well, but there are countless potential problems. If you are in business to make money, then keep it all business.

9 - Cheerfully give refunds for products that may be defective.

10 - When you don't know the answer to a customer's question, be honest and tell them you don't know. Don't make something up to cover the fact that you don't have an answer. Customers will respect you for admitting that you don't have an answer to everything, (But then be willing to say, "I'll be glad to find out for you," and follow up with the information).

How do you determine where your best markets are?

I check out what is selling at gift shops, herb stores, even malls and non-related stores. I want to see what the general public is buying this year, what trends I see, what ideas I get from watching shoppers.

One tip as to what not to sell, is to watch what the discount stores are selling. When Wal-Mart and K-Mart started selling potpourri, it was time for herb shops to either get out, or to offer something so completely different that they could still compete. When you see cows and sunflowers printed on cloth, curtains, bed sheets and towels in the discount stores, that is a tip that the public will be tired of the design very quickly, and it tells you not to order yards of material or ribbon of that design for your shop and products.

Another tip I learned from a color marketing consult with Pittsburgh Paint is when a great new color starts appearing as a choice on new cars, the color is on its way out in the next 12 months. If you see "Teal" on all the new cars in your neighborhood this year, then you better be getting rid of the teal tablecloths and ribbon in your shop because customers aren't going to be happy with products that match their car color for very long. If you want to be at the front of trends, look for indicators for what is *about* to be hot.

Target locations for selling dream pillows:

Your talents, ideas and potential may be different from another crafter's. Considering new or radically different outlets can be a creative exercise for you. If you look at markets you may have never considered, you may be surprised at what you have overlooked. Here are some places to consider for marketing your dream pillows.

• **Good quality lawn and garden shows**. Booth space can be costly at these shows, running from $500 to $1,000 or more for a 10 ft. x 10 ft. space. Unless you know your market, it probably is better to start out with a less expensive space. However, several retailers do extremely well at these shows and you might investigate the possibilities. I've sold lots of dream pillows at these kinds of shows.

• **The Internet.** I have no doubt that dream pillows can be sold well on the Internet, if the site is well designed, with lots of connections to other sites (like sci-fi sites, for instance, as well as herb sites,

gift stores, etc.). However, because dream pillows are an emotion-based product, and something that the customer likes to pick up, feel, read about, possibly smell, there are obvious limitations. There's lots of potential if you know what you're doing and room for error if you don't.

•**Herb Festivals.** We sell our dream pillows at several herb festivals and make up special blends in seasonal packages for them. The better shows require that the organizers see your products and approve them and those often have a waiting list of vendors wanting to have a booth. Look for a good show in your own area. Booth space fees of around $50-$100 are common and you can try out your marketing techniques in that setting with little cost.

•**Magazine ads.** There are advertising companies that buy up left-over ad space from all kinds of magazines each month. They, in turn, sell that space to you at a discount. You have to buy ads in several magazines at once (for instance, a fee of $300-$400 might get you word ads in a couple of astrology magazines, a new age publication and the Grit newspaper, for example). If you want to go after the dreamer-crystal-astrology market, then buying ads that way is probably the most cost effective. Otherwise, I prefer to get free publicity rather than buy it, and for complete details about how to do that, see my book, *Free Publicity* (listed with the Resources in this chapter).

•**Display ads** (which are larger and sold by the 1/8th, 1/4th, 1/2 page sizes, rather than by the column inch) are more costly. Depending upon the publication, display ad prices for a 1/4th page ad can vary from $500 to several thousand. If you have a really hot item that you know will sell vigorously, then you might consider display ads. An advantage to display ads is that there is more space and you can use graphics, to get the reader's attention. Display ads are best when run for several issues of the magazine, rather than a one-shot try. (Studies show that people must see an ad, idea or item, on average, 7 times, before it sticks in their mind!)

•**Catalogs.** A cheaper method for the small business, producing better results, is the use of your own newsletter or catalog. We send out several thousand catalogs three times a year, as well as stuffers in orders advertising specials, and we hand out more catalogs to customers who purchase something at the shows we attend. When I lecture or give a workshop, I also hand out our catalogs. Those catalogs are our best source of sales for dream pillows. (We also wholesale our pillows to shops, and have a separate catalog for those customers; call or write if you would like to order our dream pillows for your shop).

•**Craft shows.** Unless it is herbal and juried, I would stay away from those. You tend to get what I call "styrofoam egg carton crafts" at many craft fairs and those will make even your best dream pillows look cheap. Add a little dust from the hundreds of people's feet walking by, add a few children's cotton candy hands leaving their prints on your pillow packages and you can have a real dud of

Suggestion:
You might consider working with a sales representative when your products are professional and consistent. The trade and gift shows are good places to begin your search. Also trade organizations and professional trade publications sometimes have contacts with sales representatives.

Suggestion:
Be selective where you run your ads. Newspaper ads, electric cooperative magazines and regional magazines often have a poor return on ads. For example, our state electric cooperative has a circulation of about 400,000, which would lead you to think that if you get even a 3% (of readers) replying to your ad, you would do great. A classified ad will run you around $35. However, you may get 10 inquiries from a electric coop magazine ad because it's a free publication and most people throw it away without reading what's inside. A magazine like The Herb Companion, *for example, may cost you $100 for a classified ad, but you may get a 4% response/return. With a circulation of around 200,000, your money is better spent with the more dedicated readership. And the more often you run the ad, the better the responses are, in general.*

I believe the best source of publicity is the kind you get free. You may have seen us in recent issues of Southern Living, Gourmet, Country Gardens, Country Living Gardener, Garden Design *or in several Associated Press stories. It's a result of my taking my own advice from my book,* How to Get Free Publicity and Use it. *Order a copy and save yourself lots of ad costs!*

a day. Choose your shows carefully and go to the ones that have better quality crafts if you plan to make money from dream pillows.

• **Up-scale gift shops.** You might consider wholesaling your pillows to nicer gift or herb shops. Lots of craft people like making their products but hate selling them. Wholesale is a good alternative to dealing with retail customers. You might also look for a craft representative. Sometimes reps. will take on a product line, charging around 15% of sales for their fee, and they make the contacts and take the orders for you.

• **Dream Pillow parties.** I can imagine that an enterprising entrepreneur could organize a party in his or her house (women can do this best, I think). It would be like a Tupperware Party, but with Dream Pillows. Prizes, food, drawings, a casual lecture about Dream Pillows, building lots of excitement for the product, then finally, opening it up to sales for Dream Pillows and Dream Pillow books. I've never tried it, but I can see the possibilities if the right person was in charge.

Pricing

How to price the product is one of the great mysteries for the small business owner or crafts person. Most of us have a tendency to price our wares too low and that can be a fatal mistake for the business.

When pricing your product, you need to include the cost of materials, the labor, packaging, advertising and incidentals (insurance, facility, cost of your time, etc.) It isn't enough to simply look at the costs, which we'll say for our example here, of $1.00 per dream pillow. Many crafters would be happy to simply double the price and sell it for $2, feeling like they had doubled their money. But what about their time? What about time to create another product? What about investment money for more stock? Or for revenue for better advertising in order to sell more products?

The perceived value of a product should be included in your pricing formula, as well. If you make a really good product, package it well and get lots of compliments, you need to price it accordingly.

For example, in 1986, after a back injury, I sat in my garden, looking at the bounty of blooming lavender I had. I needed something to do with my hands (and something to do for money) and still allow my back to heal.

I searched my herb books and found information about making lavender wands, a craft that dates back several centuries. I taught myself how to take 17 lavender spikes and weave them with ribbon so that the lavender blossoms were inside, with a resulting object that looked something like a skyrocket.

Convinced that I had a unique and marketable craft, I made the rounds of local craft and gift stores. I priced the wands at $4.50 each and sold only a few. My friend Billy Joe took some to New

According to Richard Elia, publisher of Quarterly Review of Wines, *speaking about pricing a bottle of wine, "The more your charge, the more they (the customers) want it."*

Orleans to a craft show. On the first day of the show she priced the wands at $7.50 each and sold 5. She called me that night to ask if I cared what price she charged.

"No," I replied. "I simply need the money. Lower the price if you have to and sell as many as you can."

Her answer was, "No. Never lower the price if you have a good product. Always raise it." So she raised the price to $12.50 on the second day of the show and sold 18.

On the third day, the price was raised to $14.50 and she sold the remaining 30 wands. And when she brought the money to me, she explained about perceived value. "Price it too low and your customers think it's a poor product. Price it equal to the pride you have in your product, and you'll be successful."

Eventually I added quartz crystals that I dug myself from an Arkansas crystal mine, which I wove inside and raised the price to $36.50 each. When the price went up, I could not keep up with the demand and sold out every summer!

Look at the popularity of cigars, as another example of perceived value. They cost about 50-60¢ each to make and ship. So why do they sell for prices ranging from $7.50 to $35 on average? Because of the perceived value of the product. Cigars are popular, trendy and have a value based, not on the actual product, but on the emotional appeal. (Customers pay for looking "cool;" it's an emotionally-based product having little to do with the reality of the product). Dream pillows are in that category, too! Put them in a great package, raise the price and sell the daylights out of them!

"Never lower the price if you have a good product. Always raise it. Price it too low and your customers think it's a poor product. Price it equal to the pride you have in your product, and you'll be successful."

Billy Joe Tatum

The price of the wine is not based on the cost of the grapes.

Long Creek Herbs

Prices listed here are retail prices. If you are starting business, call us for wholesale pricing.
We offer all the supplies and materials to make and sell quality dream pillows. See the order page for complete ordering information & shipping.
Phone/Fax during normal business hours, 8-5, M-F, Central time zone: 417-779-5450.
Also order by email: Lcherbs@tri-lakes.net and from our website: **www.Longcreekherbs.com**

Dream Pillow Kits

Order these in quantity for gifts or for resale, or individually for yourself.

Each Kit includes individual packets of all of the herbs you need to make that blend, along with a cotton drawstring bag, and complete instructions for making and using your dream pillow **No sewing required!** Each kit, below, makes one pillow.

• **Pleasant Dreams Kit** - Our most popular dream blend, giving you a pleasant dream and includes herbs that help you remember your dream.

• **Restful Sleep Kit** - This herb blend is especially useful for those with nightmares or troubled sleep. Useful for adults and children. We get wonderful letters from our customers telling us how well this blend eliminates nightmares and brings restful sleep.

• **Creativity Kit** - For the person who wants vivid, colorful and enjoyable dreams. This one is a great way to encourage creativity and imagination. Lots of fun and many people who think they don't dream in color, report that their dreams are very colorful with this. (Formerly our "Action-packed" blend).

• **Romantic Kit** - For anyone who would like some spice in their dreaming. Includes herbs that have been known for centuries to evoke erotic, romantic, warm and lovingly wonderful dreaming.

Prices for individual Kits, above:
4.95 each; Order 2 for 9.00 or
Order 5 for only 21.50 and save 3.25

Our Very Best, Ready-Made Dream Pillows

Each pillow is approx. 5 x 5 inches, made of pretty cloth, filled with our own formula herb blend and padded with a bit of fiberfil. Attractively packaged and includes complete instructions for using. Order these in quantity for resale (call for wholesale pricing).

• **Pleasant Dreams Pillow** - This is our most popular dream pillow. Soothingly pleasant dreams for peaceful slumber (what we call, "Just a good dream"). This brings pleasant dreams and includes herbs for helping you remember your dreaming.

• **Restful Sleep** - This formula is especially made to ease nightmares and quieten stressful sleep. If you have trouble sleeping, or have persistent nightmares, use this one. We've had reports from parents whose children were bothered by nightmares, even Vietnam War veterans who had persisitent nightmares, all reporting restful night's sleep without nightmares! This formula is based on one taught us by a pharmacist friend many years ago.

• **Convalescent Comfort** - Physicians in past centuries used herbs in little pillows, called "comfort pillows" in the sick room to ease the discomfort felt during recuperation from illness.

• **Romantic Dreams** - This blend evokes warmly loving, slightly spicy and very romantic dreams.

• **Colorful Siestas** - An fanciful blend of herbs and exotic flowers, evoking vivid colors in warm, delightful dreams. More colorful and complex than the Creativity blend, but definitely fun for evoking creative, vivid dreams with lots of color. It's like a vacation in your dreams!

• **Creativity** - "Like reading a good book," producing pleasantly exciting, colorful dreams - one of our best for sparking creative ideas. This is our personal favorite!

• **Moon & Stars** - Filled with herbs and flowers that often produce colorful dreams of flying and gentle restfulness. Covered in extotic, dreamy cloth.

Prices for all Dream Pillows, above:
8.95 each; Order 2 for $16.50 & save $1.40
Order 4 for $32 & save $3.80
Need larger quantities?
Call for wholesale pricing.

∞Our own Formula Bulk Dream Blends∞

It's fun and easy to make your own Dream Pillows, using our Bulk Dream Blends. These are the same formulas you will find in Jim's book, *Making Herbal Dream Pillows* ($14.95, on page 2). We make the blends fresh, in small batches, using only the very best herbs and flowers. No oils or artificial ingredients whatsoever!

Note: a pound of Dream Blend is approximately 12 cups, enough to fill 16-20 deam pillows, or more, depending upon how much blend you place in each one (we recommend 2-3 tablespoons per pillow). Read specific filling instructions in our dream pillow books.

✧ Pleasant Dreams
Our most popular dream blend, gives soothingly pleasant dreams and includes herbs in the blend to help you remember your dreaming.

✧ Restful Sleep
This formula is especially made to ease nightmares and quieten stressful sleep, based on a formula first taught us by a pharmacist friend 20 years ago. Good for both adults as well as children who have trouble sleeping.

✧ Romantic Dreams
Warmly erotic, sensual and nicely romantic dreams. We get great letters from people who've used this one!

✧ Colorful Siestas
A fanciful blend that evokes vivid colors and warm, delightful dreams. More colurful and complex than the Creativity blend but definitely fun for evoking vivid dreams with lots of color.

✧ Moon & Stars
Light, airy, dreams of flying and weightlessness. It's the sweet woodruff that adds the flying aspect to this blend, and includes herbs to help the dreamer remember the dream.

✧ Creativity
This is our favorite and is the best for creativity and imaginative ideas, clarity and fantastic dreams. Fun for writers, artists, students or anyone who wants imaginative dreams.

New! ✧ Traveler's Comfort
Made especially for people who can't sleep in hotels or when they travel. Fill a little bag with 2-3 tablespoons of this blend inside and sleep on it a few nights before leaving on your trip, then take it along and sleep with it in the hotel. You'll be pleasantly surprised how this helps you sleep in unfamiliar surroundings!

New! ✧ Great Outdoors
If you enjoy the outdoors, the fragrances of nature, dreaming of hiking in the mountains and sleeping on lush carpets of forest green mosses beside crystal clear streams, this is the blend for you!

All Bulk Dream Blends
1 pound $24; 1/2 pound $14
Order 2 pounds same blend for $42

Yes, I am a dreamer.
For a dreamer is one who can only find his way by moonlight and his punishment is that he sees the dawn before the rest of the world.
— Oscar Wilde

☞ **Substitutions for Dream Flowers**
Many customers who've bought Jim's book, *Making Herbal Dream Pillows*, tell us they have difficulty finding the following flowers for dream blends. Here are suitable substitutes:
Heliotrope - use Jasmine flowers
Mimosa - *equal parts* Orange blossoms and Jasmine
Lilac - *equal parts* Linden flowers and Orange blossoms
French Marigold - use any other true marigold flower but don't substitute "pot marigold" or calendula blossoms as they are a different plant entirely. *(And don't use oils as a substitute!)*

If you can, grow mimosa, lilac & helitrope yourself and dry them in a warm, airy (but dark) place. *Microwave is not recommended.*

Unbleached Cotton Muslin Drawstring Bags
Perfect for dream pillows, bulk blends, catnip toys or other crafts.
4 x 5 inch bags, 45¢ each,
or 5 for $2
Better value: order 12 for $4.25
☞ **Best value: 100 bags for $30**

3 x 5 inch bags, 35¢ each,
or 12 for $3.60
☞ **Best value: 100 bags for $25**

Consider these for your next class or club meeting
Even more Dream Pillow choices!
We now offer you multiple-Dream Pillow Kits in several sizes
(Prices listed here do not include shipping)

Everything you need is included in each kit!

No Sewing Required!

Make Your Own
4-Dream Kit
Makes 4 Dream Pillow Gifts!

Still our most popular bulk Dream Kit, this includes all the bulk herbs, cotton drawstring bags (no sewing required) attractive gift cards and easy instructions for making 4 Dream Pillows. *Pleasant Dreams Blend.*

Dream Kit for 4......................12.95

Make Your Own
Super-8 Dream Kit
Makes 8 Dream Pillow Gifts!

The same as above, but enough herbs, cotton drawstring bags (<u>no sewing</u> required), attractive gift cards and easy instructions for making 8 delightful Dream Pillows. *Pleasant Dreams Blend.*

Dream Kit for 8......................21.95
Order 2 Super-8 Kits for $40 (that's 16 dream pillows for only $2.50 each!)

The Best Deal Yet!
Speaker's Special Kit for 25

If you're giving a class or program... this is for you!

Friends in garden and herb clubs kept asking us to put together a larger kit for their club programs. This Speaker's Special Kit includes all the bulk herbs, cotton drawstring bags, attractive gift cards and instructions to make **25 Pleasant Dream Pillows**. *(No sewing required!)*

In addition, the Speaker's Special Kit also includes:
• A complimentary copy of Jim Long's *Making Herbal Dream Pillows* book, with all the information and details about making dream pillows, a $14.95 value
• Labels for each of the herb bulk bags
• A set of specific instructions for your group to make their own dream pillows
• A list of instructions and suggestions for you, the leader, in hosting your own dream pillow program
• The kit is shipped in a table-top display box for easy use by your club or group

It couldn't be easier to host a Dream Pillows Program for your group! Great for adults, and kids, too.

Speaker's Special Kit for 25............................$39.95

Bulk Herbs for Dream Pillows & Crafts

Prices or availability may be subject to change. Note: c/s designates cut and sifted herb; whole designates the entire leaf or berry. Check or circle the amounts wanted and use this to order bulk herbs, if you wish.

Amount Herb	Amount available	$ Total
___Bay leaf, whole	1 lb. 9.50 (approx. 57 cups/lb)	___
___Calendula flowers	1 lb. 11.80; 1/2 lb. 6.25; 1/4 lb. 3.95 (approx 44 cups/lb)	___
___Catnip, c/s,	1 lb. 14.95; 1/2 lb 8.00; 1/4 lb 4.95 (approx. 20 cups/lb)	___
___Cedar leaf tips, dry	1 lb 10.30 (approx. 42 cups/lb)	___
___Cedar leaf, fresh limbs	1 lb. 8.50; 1/2 lb 4.95 (large pieces, green)	___
___Chamomile Flowers, German, 1 lb. 13.90; 1/2 lb. 7.20 (approx. 24 cups/lb)		___
___Chili Seasoning, great fragrance, outstanding flavor! 1/2 lb. 5.95, 2 for 10.50		___
___Cinnamon Sticks, 3 in. (*Cinnamomum zeylanicum*) 18.90/lb.; 1/2 lb 9.95 (approx 168 pieces/lb)		___
___Cinnamon (Cassia) whole sticks, 10 inch, AA grade 11.20 (approx 50 pieces/lb)		___
___Cloves, whole, fancy	1 lb. 6.70 (approx. 5 cups/lb)	___
___Comfrey leaf, c/s,	1 lb. 9.60; 1/2 lb. 5.80 (approx. 15 cups/lb)	___
___Damiana leaf, c/s,	1 lb. 10.30 (approx. 15 12 cups/lb)	___
___Elder flowers, whole,	1 lb. 18.90; 1/2 lb 9.95; (approx. 10 1/2 cups/lb)	___
___Eucalyptus leaf, c/s,	1 lb. 10.10; 1/2 lb 6.95 (approx. 7 cups/lb)	___
___Fennel Seed, whole,	1 lb. 5.90; half lb. 3.50; 1/4 lb 2.00 (approx 4 cups/lb)	___
___Flax seed, whole,	1 lb. 5.90; half lb. 3.50 (approx. 2 1/2 cups/lb)	___
___Frankincense,	1 lb. 16.40; half lb. 8.90; 1/4 lb. 5.20 (approx. 3 cups/lb)	___
___Ginger root, crystallized,	1 lb. 9.95 (approx. 48 pieces/lb)	___
___Hibiscus flowers, whole,	1 lb. 10.50 (approx. 9 cups/lb)	___
___Hops, Sweet,	1 lb, 14.40; half lb. 7.60; 1/4 lb. 4.00 (approx 47 cups/lb)	___
___Jasmine flowers,	1 lb. 20.40; 1/2 lb 11.00, 1/4 lb. 6.10 (approx. 28 cups/lb)	___
___Juniper berries, whole,	1 lb. 14.40 (approx. 5 cups/lb)	___
___Lavender flowers,	1 lb. 20.20, 1/2 lb. 10.50, 1/4 lb. 6.10 (approx.17 cups/lb)	___
___Leather shavings,	1 cup 3.90	___
___Lemon Balm, c/s,	1 lb 15.40, 1/2 lb. 8.00, 1/4 lb. 4.90 (approx. 20 cups/lb)	___
___Lemon peel, c/s,	1 lb 10.90 (approx. 5 cups/lb)	___
___Lemon Verbena leaf, c/s,	1 lb. 28.00, 1/2 lb. 15.50, 1/4 lb. 8.10 (approx. 7 cups/lb)	___
___Lemongrass, c/s	1 lb 6.80, 1/2 lb 3.95, 1/4 lb 2.25 (approx. 11 cups/lb)	___
___Linden flowers, whole	1 lb. 20.50 (approx. 51 cups/lb)	___
___Marjoram leaf, c/s,	1 lb 6.40, 1/2 lb. 3.95, 1/4 lb 2.00 (approx. 17 cups/lb)	___
___Mugwort, c/s,	1 lb 11.90, 1/2 lb 6.00, 1/4 lb 3.95 (approx. 21 cups/lb)	___
___Myrrh,	1 lb 19.50, 1/2 lb10.90, 1/4 lb 6.10 (approx. 2 cups/lb)	___
___Nutmeg, ground,	1 lb 9.70 (approx. 4 1/2 cups/lb)	___
___Orange Peel, c/s,	1 lb 7.90 (approx. 8 cups/lb)	___
___Orange flower petals, c/s,	1 lb 29.90, 1/2 lb 16.50; 1/4 lb 9.95 (approx. 14 1/2 cups/lb)	___
___Passion flower leaves, c/s,	1 lb 15.50 (approx. 9 1/2 cups/lb)	___
___Patchouli herb, c/s,	1 lb 20.30 (approx. 17 cups/lb)	___
___Peppermint leaf, c/s,	1 lb 7.50; 1/2 lb 4.95 (approx. 15 cups/lb)	___
___Pine, whole, fresh sprigs	1 lb. 9.95; 1/2 lb 6.95, large pieces, fresh (*inquire for availability*)	___
___Roses & petals, red,	1 lb 8.60, 1/2 lb 4.90 (approx. 20 cups/lb)	___
___Rosemary leaf, whole,	1 lb 6.40, 1/2 lb 3.80, 1/4 lb 2.00 (approx. 9 cups/lb)	___
___Sassafras root bark, c/s,	1 lb 26.00, 1/2 lb 14.10 (approx. 6 cups/lb)	___
___Sassafras green limb wood, cut, for dream pillows 4 oz. 3.00		___
___Spearmint leaf (best for dream pillows) 1 lb 6.80, 1/2 lb 3.95 (17 cups/lb)		___
___Thyme leaf, c/s	1 lb 6.50 (approx. 7 cups/lb)	___
___Vervain, blue, leaves, c/s	1 lb 14.30; 1/2 lb 8.50; 1/4 lb 4.95 (approx. 11 cups/lb)	___
___Wood Betony, c/s	1 lb 16.30; 1/2 lb 9.50; 1/4 lb 5.25 (approx. 13 cups/lb)	___
___Woodruff, sweet, c/s	1 lb 19.50, 1/2 lb 10.20, 1/4 lb 6.00 (approx. 13 cups/lb)	___

∞ Your Order ∞

Your Name _____

Shipping Address _____

City_____State_____Zip_____

Daytime Phone Number: (_____) _____

Enclose check or money order, U.S. Funds only, or use your credit card.

Your name **as it appears on your credit card** _____

We accept Visa, Mastercard & Discover *(circle one)*   Card's Expiration date _____ ____

Card #_____ - _____ - _____ - _____

Long Creek Herbs
New mailing address, same location
P.O. Box 127, Blue Eye, MO 65611
(417) 779-5450 , 9-5, M-F, Central Standard Time
We accept checks, money orders, VISA, Mastercard & Discover. We ship UPS or U.S. Postal Service. FAX orders welcome, during normal business hours (417) 779-5450.

Bulk Herbs and Bulk Blends prices subject to change; call for current pricing.

Quantity	Item	Price each	Total
		Sub-Total	
	Missouri residents only, add 5.725% sales tax..........>>>>>		
		Shipping	
		TOTAL	

Wholesale inquiries welcome

Visit our website: www.longcreekherbs.com

Packing & Shipping Charges
Minimum shipping charge............. 3.00
For orders $6.00 - $25.99, add.......... 3.50
$26.00 - $49.99, add....................... 4.50
$50.00 - $100, add......................... 5.50
Orders over $100............................ 6.50

Don't have time to do the math?
If you are paying by credit card and wish us to calculate your correct total, simply complete the top portion of this page and check the box below. We'll give you our best prices and include the receipt with your order.
Yes, please do the math & send my receipt! ☐

More Supplies for Making Dream Pillows
We stock these items to go with the dream pillows you make

Dream Pillow folder
This folder is 3 1/4 inches wide and 8 1/2 inches tall. Printed inside and out in pink and royal purple (matches the colors of *Dream Pillows & Potions* book). This makes an inexpensive gift package, when using a muslin drawstring bag filled with your dream blend (bags sold separately). Printed on heavy cardstock and has a hole punched, top and bottom for tying with your own ribbon. This is the same folder that we furnish with our Kits for 4, Kits for 8 and Kits for 25.

35¢ each
48 for $14.40
Best buy - 100 for $25

Our book, *Dream Pillows & Potions*, sells well with your dream pillows. It gives a brief background of the history of dream pillows, why they work and how to use them. It also includes some very simple dream blends (pleasant, restful, romantic). **If you are selling dream pillows be sure to offer this book to your customers.** They will buy your dream pillows, and buy the book to learn more about using dream pillows and you make an extra profit!
Retail price is $3.95.
Order 6 or more copies and your cost is only $2.25.

Suggestion:
  Include a dream pillow and our Dream Pillows book in gift baskets for Christmas and Valentine's Day. The book is printed in lavender, purple and pink and looks great in any gift assortment.

Drawstring Muslin Bags
These are perfect for Dream Pillow classes and workshops, and for use in the Dream Pillow folder,. Also perfect for catnip toys, moth-repelling herb blends and many other crafts projects.
The drawstring bags are made of unbleached muslin and each bag is ready for filling. **3 x 5 inch is the most common size used for dream pillows and fits inside the Dream Pillow folder**; 4 x 5 inch is great for other craft projects or for larger dream pillow items).

3 x 5 inch bags, 35¢ each
12 for $3.60
Best buy: 100 bags for $25

4 x 5 inch bags, 45¢ each
5 for $2
12 for $4.25
Best buy: 100 bags for $30

Great Little Herb Books by Jim Long

Jim has been a regular columnist for *The Herb Companion* magazine for eleven years and travels coast to coast with his lectures and workshops for national and regional organizations. His books have been reviewed in numerous newspapers, including *The New York Times*, *Chicago Tribune* and over 100 others. You'll find useful information and good reading in these books, and if you are in business, you'll also find that your customers love Jim's books because they are attractive, useful and inexpensive. Call for wholesale information.

Herbs, Just for Fun - *A Beginners Guide to Growing & Using Herbs* - includes designs for 3 herb gardens, propagation information and recipes for using the herbs you grow. 3.95

Herbal Cosmetics. Bountifully illustrated with Jim's drawings and old antique prints. Detailed recipes for making hair rinses, body oils, bath blends and lots more, all from the garden and kitchen. 4.95

Just for Men - This is Jim's first herbal body formula book for men. Body preparations, aftershaves and other herbal formulas, all written just for men. Humorous, useful, with lots of old-time illustations. 4.95

Classic Herb Blends - How to Make Seasonings from the Herbs You Grow with over 80 formulas for delicious seasoning blends; recipes for Mexican spice, Cajun blackened seasoning, curry, chili seasoning & lots more. You can make all these seasonings from the herbs you grow! 4.95

Recipes & Foods of the Civil War - with historical recipes, period illustrations and information about the Civil War. 4.95

Herbal Medicines on Santa Fe Trail - For the history buff, this documents many of the plants, practices and medicines of the 1840s up to the Civil War. Nicely illustrated. 4.95

Our Helpful Business Books

Written for the business owner who wants to increase earning potential from other aspects of their business. Each book is full of useful ideas, information and resources for making or saving you money.

How to Plan & Host Profitable, Successful Festivals - Written from years of experience hosting and organizing herb festivals. This book's been used by groups around the country with great letters back thanking us for the helpful, useful and profitable information. 4.95

Successful Self-Publishing - How to make money self-publishing your stories, recipes and information. Easy, step-by-step information for making money from your writing. 495

Free Publicity for Your Business or Group - Quit buying ads!. Here are the steps to getting great publicity without cost. We've had stories in *Gourmet*, *Southern Living*, hundreds of newspapers coast to coast, and been photographed by *National Geographic* & others, using the information in our book. 4.95

If you have a shop or business - we wholesale these books, too!

Making Herbal Dream Pillows
122 pages, from Storey Publishing. This book is beautiful - the illustrations alone would sell it, even if it weren't chock full of Jim's new dream blends and information (but it **is** full and beautiful). Autographed upon request. 14.95

Making Bentwood Trellises, Gates, Fences & Arbors, 144 pages. Great new designs, photos of trellises in our garden and lots of new plans for gates, fences, trellises and arbors, plant lists, tips on finding wood and more. Autographed upon request. 19.95

Photocopy this page & use it in your dream pillow display to help answer customer's questions. Sometimes customers will not ask, but prefer to read information first. I've found that this little information sheet gets customers to inquiring further and helps lead to sales.

Yes, Dream Pillows really do Work!

If a smell or fragrance, such as roses or fresh bread baking, reminds you of a pleasant memory, then dream pillows will work for you.

Dream Pillows are a craft from the 1700s. People used herbs and flowers in mixes to affect their dreams.

Dream Pillows contain quiet, subtle fragrances (they are not potpourri). The herbs have been blended for particular kinds of dreams.

Most of all, Dream Pillows are Fun!

Yes, Dream Pillows really do Work!

If a smell or fragrance, such as roses or fresh bread baking, reminds you of a pleasant memory, then dream pillows will work for you.

Dream Pillows are a craft from the 1700s. People used herbs and flowers in mixes to affect their dreams.

Dream Pillows contain quiet, subtle fragrances (they are not potpourri). The herbs have been blended for particular kinds of dreams.

Most of all, Dream Pillows are Fun!